LOSS OF PRIVILEGES

This dissertation was approved by the Rt. Rev. Edward Roelker, S.T.D., J.C.D., professor of Canon Law, as director, and by the Very Rev. John Rogg Schmidt, J.C.D., and the Rev. Romanus O'Brien, O.Carm., J.C.D., as readers.

THE CATHOLIC UNIVERSITY OF AMERICA
CANON LAW STUDIES
No. 364

Loss of Privileges

A DISSERTATION

SUBMITTED TO THE FACULTY OF THE SCHOOL OF CANON LAW OF THE CATHOLIC UNIVERSITY OF AMERICA IN PARTIAL FULFILLMENT OF THE REQUIREMENTS FOR THE DEGREE OF DOCTOR OF CANON LAW

BY

REV. JEREMIAH FRANCIS KELLIHER, S.A., A.B., S.T.L., J.C.L.
PRIEST OF THE FRANCISCAN FRIARS OF THE ATONEMENT

THE CATHOLIC UNIVERSITY OF AMERICA PRESS
WASHINGTON, D. C.
1964

NIHIL OBSTAT:

RT. REV. CLEMENT V. BASTNAGEL

Censor Deputatus

IMPRIMATUR:

✠ PATRICK A. O'BOYLE, D.D.

Archbishop of Washington

June 6, 1963

MURRAY AND HEISTER, INC.
WASHINGTON, D. C.

PRINTED BY
TIMES AND NEWS PUBLISHING CO
GETTYSBURG, PA., U. S. A.

DEDICATION

This dissertation is dedicated in humble and deep gratitude to those people whose help directly or indirectly made this dissertation possible. Those people are my parents, my religious superiors, and my professors at the Canon Law School of Catholic University.

FOREWORD

Privileges today differ widely from what they were in the time of the *Twelve Tables*. At that time a privilege was a private law; it could be either favorable or unfavorable. Later, around Cicero's time, a privilege was usually considered an unfavorable law. Gradually the meaning of the word changed until the word arrived at the stage where it always meant something favorable. Today a privilege is considered a law that confers on some person, place or thing a special favor contrary to, outside of, or also in line with existing law.

The development of the idea and the notion of privileges, as they are known today, was almost completed during the time of Gratian and Gregory IX. In the centuries that have elapsed since Gregory IX there has been very little change or development in this field, so that the legislation that is contained in the Code is, for the most part, practically the same with what is found in the Decretals of Gregory IX. Therefore this commentary has, as a sort of introduction, considered the legislation concerning the loss of privileges around the end of the twelfth century and the beginning of the thirteenth, and especially the legislation that is found in the Decretals of Gregory IX. There is also included in this historical introduction a brief study of the loss of privileges by way of revocation as found in the writings of Suarez, Castropalao, Reiffenstuel, and Schmalzgrueber.

The second part of this dissertation is devoted to a canonical commentary on "the loss of privileges," especially with reference to canons 71 to 78 in the Code of Canon Law.

The writer wishes to take this opportunity to express his gratitude to the Very Reverend Angelus Delahunt, Superior General of the Franciscan Friars of the Atonement, for the opportunity to pursue postgraduate studies in Canon Law at The Catholic University of America. The writer wishes also to express his deep gratitude to the late Monsignor Roelker for his assistance and especially his encouragement. The writer is also deeply indebted to the members of the Faculty of the School of Canon Law for their helpful suggestions and their scholarly direction and assistance in the preparation of this dissertation.

TABLE OF CONTENTS

TABLE OF CONTENTS (Continued)

CHAPTER PAGE

PART TWO

Canonical Commentary

TABLE OF CONTENTS (Continued)

PART ONE

Historical Synopsis

CHAPTER I

Legislation in the Time of the Decretals

ARTICLE 1. LOSS OF PRIVILEGES THROUGH ONE CONTRARY ACTION

One of the first ways indicated by Hostiensis (+ 1271) in his *Summa Aurea*[1] with reference to the loss of a privilege was that which derived from the performance of one contrary action. He referred to a decretal contained in the title on Constitutions in the collection of Gregory IX.[2] The basis for the decretal was taken from a decree sent by Pope Innocent III (1198-1216) to the chapter of the cathedral of Toul in the year 1207. Some of the canons of the chapter of that city had sent a notice to Pope Innocent III to inform him that he had the right to appoint a canon to a certain dignity, called *primicerius,* in the chapter of the canons, since according to the III General Council of the Lateran (1179), if an office was vacant for a certain period and was not filled by those who had the right to elect or appoint a man for the office, they then lost that right as soon as the determined period had elapsed, and then it became the exclusive right of the person's superior to make the appointment.[3]

The Pope sent some men to Toul to investigate and confirm the matter, and he also delegated them to make an appointment to the vacant office if the facts that had been related were verified. However, when the Pope's emissaries arrived, the chapter of canons informed them that the canons who sent the original

---

[1] Hostiensis (Henricus de Seguslo), *Summa Aurea* (Venetiis, 1570), lib. V, tit. 33, *de privilegio et excessibus privilegiatorum,* n. 10, *qualiter amittatur* (hereafter cited as Hostiensis).

[2] C. 8, X, *de constitutionibus,* I, 2 (Innocentius III, anno 1207).

[3] C. 2, X, *de concessione praebendae, et ecclesiae non vacantis,* III, 8 (III Lateran, 1179). Cf. Philippus Jaffé, *Regesta Pontificum Romanorum ab condita Ecclesia ad annum post Christum natum MCXCVIII* (ed. 2, correctam et auctam auspiciis Gulielmi Wattenbach curaverunt S. Loewenfeld, F. Kaltenbrunner, P. Ewald, 2 vols., Lipsiae, 1885-1888), n. 14350 (hereafter cited as Jaffé).

letter had not mentioned in their letter that they had received permission by means of a special statute, given previously by another Pope, not to have a *primicerius* appointed any more in the chapter at Toul. This information was sent back to the Pope, and he replied that, if at any time in the future they elected someone to the dignity of *primicerius,* by that one action the statute which eliminated the dignity of *primicerius* would cease to have any effect.

Accordingly, it may be concluded that certain privileges were lost through the performance of one contrary action. However, this conclusion did not hold true with reference to all privileges. The Glossator, Bernard of Parma (+ 1266), offered some opinions concerning this point.[4] The first opinion he gave was that of a certain Vincentius (+ 1248). Vincentius distinguished privileges into those that give permission to do something and those that give permission to omit something. He said that if the privilege had been given to do something, and the one who had petitioned and received the privilege did not use it for a space of ten years, then that person lost the privilege. Vincentius here referred to a rule in the *Digest* concerning the permission for public selling in a market-place, which permission, if not used for a space of ten years, would be lost.[5] If the privilege was given not to do something, or to omit doing something, and the Pope reserved to himself some right in the matter, then the privilege could not be renounced. If the Pope did not make any reservation in the matter, then the privilege was not lost until there had elapsed the time for the duration of which the privilege had been granted, or until legal prescription had taken place.

Tancredus (+ 1235), in another part of the same gloss, taught that it seems better to say that, if a privilege was given in favor of one person or of a number of individual persons, then that kind of a privilege could be lost through the performance of one contrary act. However, if the privilege was given in favor of a church or of a religious order, then that privilege was lost, not

---

[4] *Glossa Ordinaria,* c. 8, X, *de constitutionibus,* I, 2, s.v. *contravenerint.*

[5] D. (50.11) 1. *Modestinus libro tertio regularum.* Nundinis impetratis a principe non utendo qui meruit decennii tempore usum amittit.

through the performance of one contrary action, but only if the legitimate time for the operation of legal prescription had run its full course.

ARTICLE 2. LOSS OF PRIVILEGES THROUGH PRESCRIPTION

A bishop could lose his privilege of demanding tithes and funeral offerings if a prescription period of forty years had run its course against his right in these matters. Thus, Pope Alexander III (1159-1181) in writing to the Archbishop of Salerno in 1180 stated: "It seems that a cleric with respect to the fourth part of the tithes and funeral offerings can protect himself against the claim of the bishop by a prescription of forty years."[6]

The Glossator added that previously, that is, prior to the time of Justinian (527-565), a space of thirty years was a sufficient time to make legal prescription operative against a church or church property. After the time of Justinian a thirty-year prescription was still sufficient for the acquisition of private property, but a forty-year prescription was necessary with reference to church property and religious places.[7]

In a letter to Pope Alexander III sent to the Abbot and the monks of the Cistercian monastery of Saint Andrew in 1179, he informed them that they had lost their privilege of not paying tithes to the canons of a parish where the monks had some land. It was a case of prescription on the part of the canons of that parish, and a case of not making use of a privilege on the part of the monks. Through their possession of an Apostolic privilege the monks had been dispensed from paying tithes on anything they received from their own labors. However, for thirty years the monks had paid the tithes despite their privilege. Therefore, the Pope decided that the canons had acquired a right to the tithes and that the monks had at least tacitly renounced their privilege by not using it for a period of thirty years.[8]

[6] C. 4, X, *de praescriptionibus,* II, 26 (Alexander III, anno 1180); Jaffé, n. 14091.

[7] *Glossa Ordinaria,* c. 4, X, *de praescriptionibus,* II, 26, s.v. *quadragenaria;* C. 16, q. 3, *dictum post* c. 15, p. 6.

[8] C. 6, X, *de privilegiis et excessibus privilegiatorum,* V, 33 (Alexander III, 1179): Jaffé, no. 13739.

A decree which was issued in the year 1206 shows that the period of operative prescription against the Church or church property no longer was a period of only thirty years, but had increased to a period of forty years. Pope Innocent III decided a case in favor of the one for whom there was operative a legal prescription of forty years for the reception of tithes, inasmuch as the other party had at least tacitly renounced his privilege of not paying tithes for the same period. Some monks had been receiving tithes from a certain portion of land for many years. The Knights Templars then acquired the land, but continued to give the tithes to the monks who originally possessed the right of tithing for the land. After a period of at least forty years had gone by, the Knights Templars refused to pay the tithes to the monks anymore. The monks claimed they had acquired the right of receiving the tithes and the Templars lost the privilege of exemption from the tithes in consequence of a forty years' prescription. The Pope recognized the prescription as operative for the monks, but he told them that they would have to prove their statements and that in the absence of such proof they would lose their right so that the Knights would be absolved from paying the tithes.[9]

Another contemporary decretal indicated that a moral person could be liberated from certain obligations to the Holy See if a prescription period of one hundred years operated in its favor to obtain the privilege.[10]

ARTICLE 3. LOSS OF PRIVILEGES THROUGH AN ORDER OF THE HOLY SEE

The Apostolic See could take away some privileges from a diocese in order to honor some other diocese or its ruler with some special privileges.[11]

---

[9] C. 15, X, *de privilegiis et excessibus privilegiatorum,* V, 33 (Innocent III, 1206); A. Potthast, *Regesta Pontificum Romanorum inde ab anno post Christum natum 1198 ad annum 1304* (2 vols., Berolini, 1874-1875), no. 2834 (hereafter cited as Potthast).

[10] C. 13, X, *de praescriptionibus,* II, 26.

[11] C. 8, C. IX, q. 3.

The basis for this power of the Apostolic See was contained in the first rule of Pope Gregory IX, which stated that "all things are subject to dissolution by whatever gave rise to their existence."[12]

Therefore a privilege could be lost or recalled by order of the Apostolic See, since it was through the Apostolic See that these privileges came into existence.[13] The decretal stated that, if the Roman Pontiff had given a privilege *ad suae voluntatis beneplacitum,* then at the death of the Pontiff the privilege would cease. But if the privilege was given *ad Apostolicae Sedis beneplacitum,* then the privilege would not cease at the death of the Pontiff, but would continue perpetually, since the Holy See does not die. However, the same Pope or his successor still retained the power to revoke the privilege. They did revoke privileges, as will be shown later, especially when there were abuses in the use of privileges.

ARTICLE 4. LOSS OF PRIVILEGES THROUGH A CHANGE OF CIRCUMSTANCES

A privilege could also cease if in the course of time circumstances changed in such a way that the privilege would be a source of harm to the individual holding the privilege. If the privilege was harmful to an individual person who had obtained the privilege, the privilege then would cease. Among the Rules of Pope Boniface VIII (1294-1303) there was a rule that covered such a case. Rule 61 stated: "That which has been granted in one's favor ought not to be turned into one's detriment."[14]

If the privilege was a source of harm to the public good or to a third party, then it could also be revoked. In the main this resulted from a change of circumstances which rendered the privilege an unjust encroachment on the rights of others. Pope Alexander III (1159-1181) in 1180, when writing to the Abbot and the monks of a monastery in France, revoked a privilege which

---

[12] C. 1, X, *de regulis iuris,* V, 41.

[13] C. 5, 1, *de rescriptis,* I, 3, in VI°.

[14] Reg. 61, R. J., in VI°

had become harmful to the Monastery of Dol.[15] Pope Alexander wrote:

> You have brought to Our attention that the Abbot and Monks of the Monastery of Dol are seeking to withhold tithes from you. We commit it to your discretion to compose peacefully this matter with the aforesaid Abbot and Monks, for, when the Roman Church accorded to your Order the privilege of tithes, the Monasteries belonging to your Order were so few in number and so poor that no scandal could justly arise therefrom; but now they are so greatly increased in numbers and so enriched with possessions that We have received many complaints against you on this head.

In another instance, there were two monasteries for which there had arisen a dispute about an election; the monks of one monastery claimed that they had the right to have one of their monks chosen to be the Abbot of the other monastery. The Monastery of St. Bertin in Belgium claimed the privilege and contended that the monastery of St. Silvanus was bound to observe it, so that there would be chosen a monk from the monastery of St. Bertin when the election for an Abbot was held. Pope Innocent III, after having studied all the evidence, indicated that the monks of the monastery of St. Bertin did have the privilege. Since a privilege was a private law and as such accorded a special favor, therefore they still had the right to have one of their monks chosen as the Abbot of the Monastery of St. Silvanus. However, they would lose the privilege if they failed to keep up the regular observance in their monastery, or if they did not have anyone who was qualified to be placed in the Monastery of St. Silvanus as the Abbot.[16]

ARTICLE 5. LOSS OF PRIVILEGES THROUGH A DESTRUCTION OF THE PRIVILEGED OBJECT

The destruction of a privileged object seemed to include also the loss of privileges that were connected with that object. At least

---

[15] C. 9, X, *de decimis, primitiis et oblationibus,* III, 30 (Alexander III, 1180); Jaffé, n. 14004.

[16] C. 25, X, *de verborum significatione,* V, 40.

according to the Rules of Boniface VIII[17] the accessory followed the nature of the principal. If the principal had been so closely connected with the object and not merely with the place, then the privilege would cease at the destruction of the object.

In the Decretals of Gregory IX, there is a letter of Pope Gregory I (590-604) to Abbot Agapitus of the monastery of St. Marcian in Umbria concerning the privileges that were attached to a monastery in another diocese. The monastery had been destroyed by enemy action and was so completely destroyed that there must not have been any hope of rebuilding it, or at least it was not possible for the monks to continue living there. The privileges of that monastery were then transferred to another, and they were enjoyed there in the same manner as they had been in the previous monastery that had been destroyed. This seems to indicate that the destruction of a place did not necessarily mean the destruction of the privileges connected with that place.[18]

A rule regarding the loss of privileges through the destruction of the privileged object may be taken from a decree of the IV General Council of the Lateran (1215) as it is contained in the Decretals of Gregory IX.[19] It is stated at the beginning of that decretal that if the cause ceases, then the effect also ceases. In relation to privileges this referred to the principal cause or reason for which a privilege was given. Therefore the continued use of a privilege after the reason for the privilege had ceased to exist constituted an abuse of a privilege and for that reason also the holder of the privilege merited the loss of the privilege.

In like manner, if a place does not even exist, then it cannot enjoy a privilege. Thus, in a decree of Urban III (1185-1187) in 1186, it was forbidden to monasteries to ask for or enjoy privileges as monasteries until those monasteries had been canonically erected. Therefore, the privileges gained previously to the canonical erection of the monastery were of no effect and their use was forbidden.[20]

---

[17] Reg. 42, R. J. in VI°.

[18] C. 2, X, *de religiosis domibus ut espiscopo sint subjectae,* III, 36 (Gregory I, 601); Jaffé, n. 1846.

[19] C. 60, X, *de appellationibus, recusationibus et relationibus,* II, 28.

[20] C. 5, X, *de ecclesiis aedificandis vel reparandis,* II, 48 (Urbanus III, 1186); Jaffé, n. 15750.

ARTICLE 6. LOSS OF PRIVILEGES THROUGH RENUNCIATION

There are many decretals in Gregory IX's collection that speak of the loss of privileges in consequence of their renunciation. Some of these decretals show that it was forbidden in some instances to renounce a privilege; but there are others that show that, if a privilege was given to some particular person and was given for his own personal benefit and his alone, then those privileges could be lost through that person's free and express renunciation.[21]

A non-observance of the rules on prescription, or an abuse in the matter of legal prescription, could also bring about the loss of the privilege claimed in consequence of the legal prescription. A controversy mentioned in the Decretals of Gregory IX illustrates this point.[22] The case involved the monks of the Monastery of St. Martin in Hungary and the bishop of the diocese. The subject of the controversy centered on certain tithes and also on certain spiritual rights of the clerics and of the churches of that very monastery. The Abbot of the monastery petitioned the Pope to stop the bishop of that diocese from impeding them in their collecting of tithes in a certain parish. He also petitioned that the monks be permitted to look to whatever bishop they chose for the chrism, the holy oils, the reception of Holy Orders, and the consecration of their altars and churches. The Abbot had evidence to prove that the privileges concerning this matter had been obtained from Popes Alexander III (1159-1181), Paschal II (1099-1118), Clement II (1046-1047) and King Stephen (997-1038). He also could prove that they had completed the course of prescription regarding the reception of the Sacrament of Holy Orders from a bishop other than the bishop of that diocese.

The bishop of the diocese then explained the case to the Pope and showed why the tithes should be returned to him, and also why the monks should receive the sacrament of Holy Orders from him. The Pope then declared that the monks should receive the sacrament of Holy Orders from the bishop of the diocese if he was a Catholic (not a schismatic) and was willing to confer to

---

[21] C. 6, X, *de privilegiis et excessibus privilegiatorum,* V, 33.

[22] C. 19, X, *de praescriptionibus,* II, 26.

them this sacrament. Otherwise they were free to receive the sacrament of Holy Orders from any Catholic bishop whom they chose. The Pope mentioned that the prescription claimed by the Abbot regarding the sacrament of Holy Orders would not have any effect. He gave his reasons for that statement as follows: If the monks petitioned from a Pope a privilege that was contrary to the privilege they had obtained through legal prescription, then they renounced the privilege obtained through prescription. If the legal prescription had not run its full course when they petitioned for the contrary privilege, then the prescription would have been continued in bad faith, and therefore as a result there was no prescription.

It was forbidden for a cleric to renounce his *privilegium fori* and to submit to corporeal punishment for some offense or crime he may have committed. Pope Innocent III in 1214 declared that the privilege was not just for the cleric, but for the whole clerical state, and the individual cleric was not permitted to renounce the privilege. If he did renounce the privilege after this prohibition, he was to be excommunicated.[23]

However, the cleric lost all the privileges of the clerical state if he no longer wore the clerical habit or tonsure, and if after receiving three warnings concerning his actions he still refused to reform by returning to the practice of the clerical state.[24]

In like manner religious were also forbidden to renounce their privilege of exemption without the permission of the Holy See.[25]

Pope Innocent III in 1206 condemned the practice of the Archbishop of Pisa, whereby clerics were permitted to renounce the *privilegium fori* by selecting a lay judge to try their cause. The Pope reminded the Archbishop that a cleric as a private individual had no right to renounce that which was a public right of the clerical state. The *privilegium fori* was a privilege which had been given to the entire clerical state, and therefore it could not be renounced by a private individual.[26]

---

[23] C. 36, X, *de sententia excommunicationis* V, 39 (Innocent III, 1214); Potthast, n. 2693.

[24] C. 45, X, *de sententia excommunicationis,* V, 39; Potthast, n. 4641.

[25] C. 5, X, *de arbitris,* I, 43 (Innocent III, 1198); Potthast, n. 327.

[26] C. 12, X, *de foro competenti,* II, 2 (Innocent III, 1206); Potthast, n. 2769.

ARTICLE 7. LOSS OF PRIVILEGES THROUGH HERESY

In the twelfth or thirteenth century, there did not exist the separation of Church and State as it is found in most countries in the twentieth century. In the Middle Ages, the State co-operated with the Church in defense of the dogmas of Faith, and also co-operated in the punishment of those who committed crimes against the Church or its dogmas. Heresy, therefore, was considered a public crime and punishable in law. The Church authorities passed judgment on a person convicted of heresy. If the charge was substantiated, the sentence of excommunication was imposed. If the guilty person did not reform and make an abjuration of his heresy, then, if he was a cleric, he was reduced to the lay state, and, if a layman, he was deprived of all his privileges and turned over to the civil authorities to be punished. Even those whom suspicion rightly fell upon were subjected to the same treatment. Likewise, if the secular rulers refused to defend the Church against heretics, they could be excommunicated and their lands put under interdict. If a city refused to punish its citizens who were heretics and, if it was admonished by its bishop and still refused to carry out its duties, then that city could be deprived of the trade and communication with the other cities around it, and also the dignity held by the city as an episcopal see could be removed. Finally, all those who enjoyed the privilege of exemption and were subject only to the Holy See were nevertheless also subject to the local ordinary in the matters that pertained to heresies and their punishment. The local ordinary was considered a delegate of the Holy See when he dealt with matters that pertained to heresies, heretics, and persons suspected of heresies. These regulations were contained in a letter of Pope Lucius III (1181-1185), which he wrote in 1181.[27]

ARTICLE 8. LOSS OF PRIVILEGES THROUGH THEIR ABUSE

One of the main causes for bringing about the loss of privileges was their abuse. And their abuse could arise from many different sources. In a letter sent by Pope Gregory IX (1227-1241) to the

[27] C. 3, X, *de haereticis,* V, 7 (Lucius III, 1181).

Bishop of Paris in 1229,[28] the Pope described some of the abuses that were prevalent at that time in the obtaining of privileges. He deprived the guilty ones of the privileges and benefits mentioned in the rescripts, and these same people were also forced to pay any expenses or damages that befell any third party because of the use of those privileges. One of the first abuses named was that of someone getting a rescript in his own name and of then giving it to someone else who had the same name. Or, perhaps some rescript was used in some controversy which did not even exist at the time the rescript was petitioned. Or, again, a defendant had a plaintiff cited at one and the same time to many different places, or, to a small town with a name that was common to small towns in a number of provinces in the same area, and if the plaintiff did not appear, the defendant had him judged contumacious.

Pope Innocent III (1198-1216) ordered that a privilege which certain clerics had enjoyed be taken away when they were subjecting the privilege to abuse. The privilege granted certain clerics the right to obtain the revenues from non-residential benefices whenever these clerics could not reside at the place of their benefice and at the same time pursue their studies. The Pope had granted the privilege to encourage the clerics in their literary pursuits. However, the clerics used the privilege to take vacations or to go to places where very few if any academic interests were followed, or at least there were fewer such interests in those places as compared with the place where their benefice existed. Therefore, since no one was to obtain any revenues from a benefice through fraud or deceit, the clerics lost the use of the privilege. This ruling was contained in a letter to the Bishop of Auxerre, France, in 1207.[29]

ARTICLE 9. LOSS OF PRIVILEGES THROUGH THEIR UNAUTHORIZED USE

Another abuse of privileges that Pope Innocent III sought to correct was that of the unauthorized use of privileges. Some monks had been extending the privilege of exemption to chapels which

[28] C. 43, X, *de rescriptis,* I, 3 (Gregorius IX, 1229) ; Potthast, n. 9538.

[29] C. 12, X, *de clericis non residentibus in ecclesia vel praebenda,* III, 4 (Innocent III, 1207) ; Potthast, n. 3105.

indeed were under their care, but which did not form part of the Monastery of Evesham which enjoyed the privilege of exemption. In the beginning of a letter sent to the Abbot and the Monks of the monastery in question, Pope Innocent described his position. He said: "From the mouth of the One sitting on the Throne proceeds a two-edged sword,[30] since from the mouth of the Roman Pontiff the most upright judgments must proceed, which can in no way offend against justice, but must render to each one his due. Therefore just as the papal authority will defend someone's privilege, in like manner it will take away a privilege that has been unjustly assumed by some party."

In this particular case, one monastery was given the privilege of exemption and put under the special protection of the Archbishop of Canterbury. The monks of this monastery then extended the privilege of exemption to another house in the diocese of Worcester. The Bishop of the diocese of Worcester objected. The case was sent to Rome for the decision of the Pope. Pope Innocent condemned the practice of extending the privilege beyond those for whom the privilege was granted and commanded the monks to show reverence, obedience and respect to the Bishop of Worcester.[31]

ARTICLE 10. LOSS OF PRIVILEGES THROUGH MISCONDUCT AND CRIME

There are many instances in the Decretals of Gregory IX that give evidence of the fact that clerics who had committed crimes, or who had been guilty of some misconduct, were deprived of some or all of their privileges, and in some instances were also punished by the civil authorities.

The Archbishops and Bishops at the III General Council of the Lateran in 1179 were warned by Pope Alexander III (1159-1181) to stop interfering with the privileges of the Knights Templars, or they would be deprived of their own privileges.[32]

---

[30] Apoc., I, 16.

[31] C. 17, X, *de privilegiis et excessibus privilegiatorum,* V, 33 (Innocent III, 1206); Potthast, n. 2660.

[32] C. 4, X, *de privilegiis et excessibus privilegiatorum,* V, 33 (Alexander III, 1179); Jaffé, n. 13961.

In the same Council it was decreed that if anyone was elected invalidly to the papacy and tried to assume the office, both he and all those who co-operated with him would be excommunicated and deprived of all their privileges, of the exercise of their sacred orders, and of the reception of the sacraments, except Viaticum if they were dying.[33]

Clement III in 1190 deprived clerics, if they had volunteered for military service, of all their clerical privileges if after three warnings they still persisted in remaining in the military service.[34]

In 1220, Honorius III (1216-1227) decreed that all clerics who had married were deprived of their clerical privileges.[35]

The same Pope Honorius decreed that all clerics who engaged themselves in secular businesses and neglected the obligations of the clerical state, or the obligations attached to their benefice, were to be deprived of all their clerical privileges if, after three warnings, they refused to give up the secular business they were engaged in.[36]

ARTICLE 11. SOME RULES OF LAW THAT AFFECTED THE LOSS OF PRIVILEGES

a) If a privilege was held *in forma accessoria,* it was one with the privilege held *in forma principali.* It was the same privilege, no matter how it was held. Therefore, since it was one and the same privilege, it was increased, decreased, or lost if for the principal agent it was increased, decreased or lost.[37]

b) Boniface VIII said in his rules: "That which has been granted in one's favor ought not to be turned into one's detriment."[38]

---

[33] C. 6, X, *de electione et electi potestate,* I, 6.

[34] C. 25, X, *de sententia excommunicationis,* V, 39 (Clement III, 1190); Jaffé, n. 16574.

[35] C. 9, X, *de clericis coniugatis,* III, 3 (Honorius III, 1220); Potthast, n. 5755.

[36] C. 16, X, *de vita et honestate clericorum,* III, 1 (Honorius III, 1218); Potthast, n. 5784.

[37] C. 1, X, *de regulis iuris,* V, 41; Reg. 42, R. J., in VI°.

[38] Reg. 61, R. J., in VI°.

The same idea was expressed in a decretal to be found in Gregory IX's collection. In referring to a privilege which was given to some monks, but which they did not use, the Pope stated that everyone was free to renounce his rights.[39] But the renunciation spoken of could be understood in the sense that it was not absolutely renounced for all time, but rather that its use was deferred for a time. However, if that time was extended beyond a certain period established by the donor of the privilege, the recipient could lose the privilege through its non-use.[40] However, if a privilege, when granted to a private individual, was meant for the benefit of a community, or a place, or a thing, then the individual could not renounce the privilege, and he had to make use of it. Therefore a cleric could not forego the use of his *privilegium fori*.[41]

c) A subsequent privilege could cancel out the privileges mentioned in an earlier rescript, if the later rescript stated that fact.[42] And a subsequently granted special privilege enjoyed priority over a general one. Pope Innocent III in 1204 wrote to the Bishop of Ely, England, that beyond all doubt a special rescript prevailed over a general one, and that any authority attaching to a general rescript was taken away completely through a special rescript (but only in those matters that were expressed as special), even though it did not mention the prior rescript.[43]

According to the Rules of Boniface VIII, a personal privilege followed the person everywhere, and also ceased at the death of the one holding the privilege.[44]

---

[39] C. 6, X, *de privilegiis et excessibus privilegiatorum*, V, 33 (Alexander III, 1179); Jaffé, n. 13739.

[40] C. 15, X, *de privilegiis et excessibus privilegiatorum*, V, 33 (Innocent III, 1206); Potthast, n. 2834.

[41] C. 2, X, *de mutuis petitionibus*, II, 4 (Celestine III, 1193); Jaffé, n. 17019; C. 12, X, *de foro competenti*, II, 2 (Innocent III, 1206); Potthast, n. 2769; C. 23, X, *de regularibus et transeuntibus ad religionem*, III, 31 (Gregory IX, 1227-1234); Potthast, n. 9650.

[42] C. 31, X, *de privilegiis et excessibus privilegiatorum*, V, 33 (Gregory IX, 1227-1234); Potthast, n. 9681.

[43] C. 14, X, *de rescriptis*, I, 3 (Innocent III, 1204); Potthast, n. 2350.

[44] Reg. 7, R. J., in VI°.

However, a privilege was not necessarily lost if the person who granted the privilege had died or had discontinued his tenure of office. This was true especially regarding the privileges given by the popes. Some privileges were given with the understanding that they would cease when the pope died or when he no longer wished that person or persons to have some privilege. Other privileges continued even after the death of the pope who had granted the privilege, and these lasted permanently until some future pope decided to recall the privilege.[45]

---

[45] C. 5. *de rescriptis,* I, 3, in VI°.

CHAPTER II

Jurisprudential Developments

In the previous chapter, a short conspectus of the legislation of the Church concerning the loss of privileges according to the Decretals of Gregory IX was set forth. There were enumerated the many different ways by which privileges were lost. In this chapter a brief study will be made of the loss of privileges by way of revocation as found in the writings of Suarez, Castropalao, Reiffenstuel, and Schmalzgrueber.

From the history of privileges during the time after the decretalists until and including the Council of Trent, it was quite evident that the Holy See could and did revoke many privileges, especially those of the religious orders. Pope Boniface VIII published in the year 1300 the Constitution *Super cathedram,* in which he set down certain rules in matters of preaching, of hearing confessions, and of granting burials, and revoked all the privileges of the Friars in so far as they militated against the provisions of his Constitution. His successor, Benedict XI, abrogated this Constitution in the year 1304.[1]

However, the results were disastrous, so that Pope Clement V (1305-1314), at the requests of the bishops, restored the Constitution at the third session of the Council of Vienne (1311-1312). The Constitution read in part:

> All privileges, favors and immunities, verbal or written in any form, expression, or conception of words, granted by us or by our predecessors, the Roman Pontiffs, to the aforesaid orders, as well as all customs, agreements and decisions in so far as they militate against the foregoing provisions or against any of them, we revoke and declare absolutely null and void.[2]

---

[1] C. 1, *de privilegiis, V, 7, in Extravag. com.*

[2] Canon 2 of the Council of Vienne; Schroeder, *Disciplinary Decrees of the General Councils: Text, Translation, and Commentary* (St. Louis: Herder, 1937), p. 382.

At the V General Council of the Lateran (1512-1517) the privileges of the religious once again came under the criticism of the bishops. Pope Leo X (1513-1521) issued the Bull, *Dum intra mentis arcana,*[3] which revoked some privileges and abolished others that were among the privileges enjoyed by most religious and known as the *Mare Magnum.*

The Council of Trent (1545-1563) in its twenty-fifth reform session also revoked certain privileges listed in the collection known as the *Mare Magnum.* However, most of these privileges were revoked because they had become useless or even harmful.[4]

[3] Sessio XI, 19 dec. 1516—Jean Hardouin, *Acta Conciliorum et Epistolae Decretales ac Constitutiones Summorum Pontificum* (12 vols., Parisiis, 1714-1715), IX, 1832-1835.

[4] Sessio XXV, Chapter 22, Council of Trent; Schroeder, *Canons and Decrees of the Council of Trent* (St. Louis: Herder, 1941), p. 231.

SECTION I

Revocation of Privileges According to Suarez and Castropalao

Article 1. Revocation of Generous Privileges

Castropalao (1581-1633) taught that the revoking of a generous privilege by the one who granted the privilege or by his successor connoted at least a venial sin if the privilege was revoked without any cause or reason.[5] By a generous privilege Castropalao meant a privilege that was given to someone in a gratuitous manner without consideration being given to the merits of that person. It was not given as a form of a reward for services rendered. Therefore the reason for the granting of a generous privilege was the pure liberality of the grantor, and not the merit of the one who received the privilege.[6]

A generous privilege, according to Castropalao, could be revoked and revoked validly. According to his opinion a person who held a generous privilege was in the same position as a person who has been given a delegation. And since a delegate remains subject to the will of the delegating person, in like manner a privileged person remains subject to the will of the one who granted the privilege in those matters that pertain to the privilege. Therefore if the one who granted the privilege wanted to revoke the privilege he could do so in the same manner as a principal agent could revoke the powers he had granted to his delegate.[7]

Secondly, according to the same author, if a superior granted to some subject a privilege that permitted him to act against the common law, the granting of that privilege did not remove that subject from his jurisdiction. Therefore the superior could exercise that jurisdiction by once again imposing on that person the

---

[5] Castropalao, *Opus Morale* (2 vols., Lugduni, 1682), I, tr. 3, disp. 4, p. 21, n. 1 (hereafter cited as Castropalao).

[6] *Ibid.*, n. 3.

[7] *Ibid.*, n. 4.

precept from which he was excused through the privilege. However, this was not to be done without a reason or cause, since to change one's will without cause could be a sign of levity and inconstancy and against the nature of a good ruler, since it is fitting that these things remain permanent.[8]

If the generous privilege granted a person ownership or dominion over something, then that privilege could not be revoked without a legitimate reason. Otherwise, someone could, without a cause or reason, be deprived of the very things he owns which is contrary to the whole notion of ownership.[9]

Castropalao also stated that compensation was not required in justice when a person, for a just reason, was deprived of his generous privilege. The reason for this was that the privilege itself had been freely given and accordingly followed the rules on gifts, namely, that they could be revoked without compensation when a just reason was present. Furthermore, the one granting a generous privilege did not give up his right to revoke this privilege if a just reason arose, or also to do this without making any compensation.[10]

Suarez (1548-1617) offered an objection to the revocation of privileges by saying that a privilege was like a gift: once a gift had been made to a person it could not be taken back, and similarly a privilege, once it had been accepted, could not be revoked.[11]

Suarez saw the need for making a distinction between privileges granted to those who are subjects and privileges granted to those who are not subjects. Privileges granted to those who are not subjects could not, when accepted by them, be revoked by the one who had granted the privileges. Suarez explained that a privilege granted to a non-subject and accepted by him became in a sense a contract, and therefore could not be revoked except upon a mutual agreement. Just as a ruler has no right to deprive non-subjects of things that belong to them when legitimately acquired,

---

[8] *Loc. cit.*

[9] *Ibid.,* n. 6.

[10] *Ibid.,* n. 7.

[11] Suarez, *Opera Omnia* (28 vols., editio nova a Carolo Berton [Vols. V and VI, *De Legibus et Legislatore Deo*], Parisiis, 1856-1861). VI, lib. VIII, cap. 37, n. 1, p. 405 (hereafter cited *De Legibus*).

in the same manner he cannot revoke the privileges he has granted to non-subjects when freely accepted by them. The privilege simply did not any longer come under the domain of the grantor.

However a generous privilege granted to a subject could be revoked by the one who granted the privilege. Whenever a legitimate cause was present and it was morally necessary, a superior could revoke a generous privilege possessed by his subject in the same way in which he could, with just cause, deprive him of some right or some thing over which he had dominion. It also seemed to Suarez that compensation in these instances was really not necessary. The privilege was freely given and the one granting it did not oblige himself to the non-revoking of the privilege, especially if a legitimate cause was present, or to the revoking of the privilege only upon a previous corresponding compensation. The one granting the privilege would hardly have granted the privilege under other conditions.[12]

Accordingly, Suarez concluded that a generous privilege, when granting permission or faculties to act contrary to or outside of the common law, could freely be revoked by the one granting it, as long as some necessity demanded it and it was being revoked from some subject. He pointed out that the Glossators explained this by saying that these generous privileges never really came under the dominion of the holder of the privilege, and therefore always depended upon the will of the one granting the privilege. It worked the same way as a precept. A superior could take away a precept, but then could impose it again, or he could give a precept, and later on take it away. Therefore the pope on granting a dispensation for a matrimonial impediment could later also revoke it before the contracting of the marriage. But if the pope had dispensed someone from a vow he could not revoke the dispensation, since he could not repair the bond of the vow and likewise could not command the person to make the vow again. According to the mind of Suarez a superior could without doubt effectively revoke such generous privileges as he had granted to his subjects, even when he acted without a warranting reason.

---

[12] *Ibid.*, nn. 4, 9, 10, pp. 406-408.

But if the revocation was undertaken without a reason, then its lawfulness, though not its validity, could be called into question.[13]

ARTICLE 2. REVOCATION OF ONEROUS AND REMUNERATIVE PRIVILEGES

According to Castropalao an onerous privilege was a privilege granted by means of a contract or agreement whereby the person receiving the privilege was under the obligation to pay a certain price or perform a certain work. A remunerative privilege was a privilege granted to someone as a reward or satisfaction for work done, or in recognition of the special merits of a particular person.

Castropalao held that when onerous privileges were granted under seal of contract (*per contractum*), that is, with the accompanying obligation of paying some price or of performing some work, they could not be revoked without a just cause. Such a just cause could be constituted only by the common good or by a public utility. Also, if the one who granted the privilege accepted some price for it, then he had to return the same if he revoked the privilege. In like manner, if work was done for the obtaining of the privilege, then compensation was to be made for the work done. Otherwise, as Castropalao contended, the revocation was null as well as unjust.[14]

Suarez contended that privileges which persons acquired by paying a certain price could not be revoked by the one who granted the privilege, because to do so would offend against natural justice by depriving a person of his own property. Only in a very rare case could such a revocation be rightfully made, as when public necessity or some other urgent reason demanded that this person be deprived of his privilege. But in all of these cases the due compensation was to be made.[15]

According to this doctrine, said Castropalao, any dispensation from marriage impediments given by the Holy Father in the ex-

---

[13] Suarez, *De Legibus,* lib. VIII, cap. 37, nn. 7, 10,—*Opera Omnia,* VI, 407-408.

[14] Castropalao, I, tr. 3, disp. 4, p. 21, n. 2.

[15] Suarez, *De Legibus,* lib. VIII, cap. 37, n. 5,—*Opera Omnia,* VI, 406.

ternal forum could not be revoked by him unless a just cause was present and the money (*pretium*) paid for the privilege or the dispensation was returned. Castropalao also remarked that, when the Jubilee Indulgences were announced in 1624, the Holy Father indicated his revocation of all other privileges and faculties of that kind that had been granted to individual persons, no matter what their rank, or for what reason they had been granted the privileges. However, Castropalao contended that in the case of the Crusaders they had been granted special privileges for the work they had done, or had vowed to do, and that therefore, until they were mentioned specifically and compensation had been made for the work done, the revocation would be null and unjust.[16]

Castropalao taught that what was said about the revocation of onerous privileges applied in like manner to remunerative privileges. This was true whether these were given out of justice or by way of pure gratuity, for the privileged person had a right to these privileges as to something that was owed to him.[17] With reference to these remunerative privileges the question was asked whether the consideration of the public good provided a sufficient warrant for the revocation, or whether there also was due a certain remuneration, as in the case of the onerous privileges. Suarez said there was need of remuneration even when the remuneration was postulated solely out of gratitude and not simply out of justice. He felt that the remunerative privilege was in the same category as the onerous privilege, since the benefit of the privilege could be estimated at a certain price, and the loss of the privilege was certainly a hardship to the one who had held the privilege. He felt, therefore, that it was not only necessary that the public good demand the revocation of a remunerative privilege, but likewise there had to be some kind of compensation to the privileged person for the loss of the remunerative privilege.[18]

Suarez also held that a remunerative privilege given out of justice became irrevocable.[19] He came to this conclusion upon

---

[16] Castropalao, I, tr. 3, disp. 4, p. 21, n. 2.

[17] *Loc. cit.*

[18] Suarez, *De Legibus*, lib. VIII, cap. 37, n. 6,—*Opera Omnia*, VI, p. 406.

[19] *Loc. cit.*

showing that a remunerative privilege was a contract in the wide sense of the term. He claimed that a contract was involved, since what was given in remuneration was considered not as given freely, but as given in consequence of an obligation. And what was given under obligation could not be revoked in the future if the one receiving the privilege actually fulfilled the conditions of the contract. The same was to be said for a privilege given for work done. Whenever the privilege was given as payment of a just debt, then there was no doubt that it was irrevocable. But when the sole reason for granting the privilege was gratitude for something done, then the laws concerning contracts did not bind in the case. And therefore, all things being equal, the remunerative privilege given simply out of gratitude could be considered revocable, whereas the remunerative privilege given out of justice could not.

ARTICLE 3. THOSE WHO CAN REVOKE GENEROUS, ONEROUS AND REMUNERATIVE PRIVILEGES

The one granting the privilege and also his successor could revoke the granted privilege. This was true even when it was the Holy Father who had given the original privilege.

But could a subordinate, if he had been granted the power of dispensing or of granting privileges against the law of the superior, revoke the dispensations or privileges that he himself had given? Suarez taught that in such a case a subordinate could revoke the privileges he had granted. He insisted that a subordinate could do this validly even without a legitimate reason, though such an action would be lacking in prudence. The reason was based on the manner in which the privilege was given. The dispensation cancelled out the law of the superior, not absolutely indeed, but rather dependently on the will of the person granting the privilege, or by means of the tacit condition that this privilege should last until the grantor ordered otherwise or until he revoked it. This condition, although not expressed, seemed to be intrinsically included as long as it was not positively excluded.[20]

[20] *Ibid.*, n. 15, p. 409.

Castropalao felt that more probably a subordinate could not validly revoke any dispensation given by himself in reference to the law of his superior, unless he had a compelling reason for so doing.[21] Therefore, the bishop could not without a compelling reason revoke the permission given to a pastor of not residing in the place of his benefice, since it was a dispensation from the law of the bishop's superior. After the bishop had dispensed from that law he could not again apply the law. In like manner the Sacred Penitentiary, without a good reason, could not revoke dispensations already granted.

The Holy Father could revoke validly, even without a just reason, any dispensation given by any prelate subject to him, and could once again apply the law with reference to which the dispensation had been granted, and make that person subject to it once again. However, no other prelate, so it seemed to Castropalao, could revoke dispensations given by any subordinate prelate, since it would have been unjust to deprive the subordinate prelate of the legitimate use of his ordinary jurisdiction.[22]

Suarez supported the opinion that a privilege granted by a subordinate could be revoked validly and licitly by a superior if a just cause was present. He stated that just as a superior could revoke the law of a subordinate, since he held a higher jurisdiction to which the subordinate was subjected, so also could he revoke a privilege given by a subordinate as long as a just cause was present.[23]

But, if a just cause was not present, then Suarez doubted if the superior could revoke the privileges granted by a subordinate. If it could be done validly, it would still militate against the proper order of things, so that injury to the subordinate prelate and a certain detriment to the subjects would result.

ARTICLE 4. DIFFERENT MEANS BY WHICH PRIVILEGES WERE REVOKED

Castropalao pointed out that there are two types of revocation: express revocation and tacit revocation. The express revocation

---

[21] Castropalao, I, tr. 3, disp. 4, p. 21, n. 3.

[22] *Loc. cit.*

[23] Suarez, *De Legibus*, lib. VIII, cap. 37, n. 17,—*Opera Omnia*, VI, p. 410.

was effected by means of words that signified a revocation of the privilege. The tacit revocation was effected by means of an action which made it impossible for someone to make use of his privilege.[24]

The express revocation was usually effected by means of a general clause attached to the grant of some new privilege that was being given, if therein it was stated that this privilege was valid and had force notwithstanding any privilege to the contrary. However, unless there was also added a clause concerning onerous or remunerative privileges, it was not presumed that these were revoked, for such a revocation would have militated against the rights of third parties, unless the public good was involved and compensation was made for the loss brought about as a result of the revocation. Suarez stated that the decree of revocation at least had to contain the clause that certain privileges were revoked even when they had been granted on a contractual basis.[25] He explained that in ordinary law these privileges are irrevocable, and that there would have to exist a very grave reason before they could be revoked. Accordingly it was not to be presumed that they were revoked, unless such a reason had been indicated.

Castropalao held also that some privileges contained a clause in which it was stated that specific mention had to be made of them before they were revoked. But the competent superior could meet this requisite condition by adding to the new privilege such a clause as: all privileges to the contrary are revoked, even if they contain a clause which states they cannot be revoked unless specific mention is made of them.[26]

Suarez also held that a general clause was not sufficient for revoking any privileges that were granted with the condition that they could not be revoked unless special mention had been made of them. However, he was also of the opinion that it would be possible to add to the new privilege another clause revoking all privileges contrary to this new one, even though they state that special mention must be made of them before they are revoked.

---

[24] Castropalao, I, tr. 3, disp. 4, p. 21, n. 4.

[25] Suarez, *De Legibus,* lib. VIII, cap. 38, n. 3,—*Opera Omnia,* VI, p. 411.

[26] Castropalao, I, tr. 3, disp. 4, p. 21, n. 4.

Otherwise the pope would be forced to examine every privilege given out and the manner in which it was given in order to be sure that all the contrary privileges were revoked. This would be impracticable and impossible, for it would prevent him from revoking privileges even though there might be a real necessity for doing so.[27]

Another exception to the rule, namely that a general clause usually sufficed for revoking all contrary privileges when added to a new privilege, looked to that group of privileges which were contained in the main part of a law. These privileges were not revoked by means of any general clause. The revocation had to mention the law or the canon. In like manner, if a privilege had been granted by a general council and later was being revoked, express mention had to be made that this new privilege was valid notwithstanding any existing contrary privileges, even if given by a general council. Therefore, if some privilege was granted against some law or council, that privilege would not be valid unless a derogatory clause mentioned the law or the council at least in a general way.[28] Castropalao felt that a specific mention of the earlier council itself would not be necessary.[29]

According to Castropalao, even if the Pope failed to expressly mention in his derogatory clause the contrary constitution of a general council, as long as his intentions were clear, and provided that it had been his usual custom and practice to grant some certain privilege, such as a dispensation from the impediment of affinity, the privilege would be valid notwithstanding the contrary constitution of a general council.[30]

If the revocation was not indeed express but simply tacit, did the earlier granted privilege remain if a second privilege contrary to the first was issued? Castropalao held that, if an express revocation was not incorporated in the new privilege, then the benefits of the first privilege, as long as they were not contrary to the

[27] Suarez, *De Legibus,* lib. VIII, cap. 38, nn. 1-2, pp. 410-411.—*Opera Omnia,* VI, pp. 410-411.

[28] Castropalao, I, tr. 3, disp. 4, p. 21, n. 4.

[29] *Loc. cit.*

[30] *Loc. cit.*

second privilege, remained. Therefore, only the part that was contrary was to be considered as abrogated. Abrogation was to be considered an odious thing, especially with reference to privileges, and therefore it was to be restricted as much as possible.[31]

Suarez explained that a tacit revocation existed when the lawgiver placed some act which could not have any effect without revoking a previous privilege. The previously granted privilege was to be considered revoked when the new act completely covered the matter dealt with in a previous privilege, and the one granting the later privilege knew of the earlier existing privilege and the conflict between the two, but notwithstanding wanted the latter action to be placed. Suarez admitted that the difficulty in certifying the existence of a tacit renunciation hinged on whether or not the lawgiver who placed the later act knew of the previous privilege.[32]

Castropalao stated that the second granted privilege did not abrogate a prior granted privilege unless the grantor had some kind of knowledge of the earlier existing privilege. But when could it be presumed that the grantor of a privilege had knowledge of the previous privilege, and also had the intention of abrogating it? The difficulty in reaching a decision on this point was increased when in opposition to the earlier privilege there was issued simply a later privilege which abstracted from all mention of the earlier privilege.[33]

Castropalao pointed out three cases in which it might be difficult to decide whether or not a privilege has been revoked, and then he suggested how this dilemma could be solved in each case. The three cases were exemplified in the passing of a general law contrary to a prior privilege; in the granting of a privilege which as contrary to other privileges nevertheless did make mention of them, and, lastly, in the rendering of a judgment against a prior privilege. In the first case, so he stated, whenever a general law was enacted without a derogatory clause, then the prior privileges contrary to the privileges enacted in the new general law could

---

[31] Castropalao, I, tr. 3, disp. 4, p. 21, n. 5.

[32] Suarez, *De Legibus*, lib. VIII, cap. 38, n. 6, p. 412,—*Opera Omnia,* VI, p. 412.

[33] Castropalao, I, tr. 3, disp. 4, p. 21, n. 5, § 9.

be considered abrogated if they had formed part of the very law which was being abrogated by the later general law. The reason for this derived from the presumption that the lawgiver knew both what was in the law he was promulgating and what was in the law he abrogated by means of his new general law. However, if the privilege which was to be abrogated by means of the new general law had received mention only in a special or particular law, then the abrogation as deriving through the new general law was not to be presumed, since what was contained in a special or particular law could readily have escaped the knowledge of the lawgiver, and therefore would not be abrogated or revoked by his general law for the simple lack of his advertence to it.[34]

The second method by means of which a prior privilege was revoked, even though no derogatory clause appeared, was through the granting of another privilege. But here a distinction was made by Castropalao. If the prior privilege had been mentioned in a law, then it was abrogated in so far as it was contrary to the second privilege, even though there was no mention of the abrogation of the prior privilege. The reason for this was to be found in the principle that the grantor of a privilege was presumed to know the laws that existed, and accordingly also the privileges enacted in those laws. Therefore, whether the new privilege was granted as a special or as a general privilege, or whether it did or did not receive mention in the later law, imported no difference. As long as the previous privilege was enacted in some general law, it could be presumed that the grantor knew about it when he issued a second privilege contrary to the first. Since he knew about it and still intended to grant the second privilege, it could be presumed that he gave the second privilege with a tacit derogatory clause revoking the first privilege.[35]

But if there was given a privilege contrary to a previous privilege, and if no mention was made of the previous privilege, and if that privilege did not exist as part of any law, then it was not presumed to be revoked through the subsequent privilege. This

[34] Castropalao, I, tr. 3, disp. 4, p. 21, n. 5, § 10; Suarez, *De Legibus*, lib. VIII, cap. 39, n. 2,—*Opera Omnia*, VI, p. 412.

[35] Suarez, *ibid.*, nn. 2, 5, pp. 412-413; Castropalao, *ibid.*, n. 5, § 11.

would be true if both privileges were general, or if both were special, or if the first one was special and the second one was general. It was presumed in these circumstances that the one granting the second privilege did not know of the existence of the first. Castropalao referred to a decretal of Boniface VIII,[36] in which it was decided that a privilege given to the Cistercians was not revoked through a subsequent privilege in which no mention had been made of the prior privilege of the Cistercians.[37]

When the first privilege was a general or a universal one, and the second privilege was a special or a particular one, then the first privilege still prevailed, since knowledge of this privilege was not to be presumed unless this privilege had received mention in a law, nor was it to be presumed that the grantor of a privilege wished to revoke the privileges of another unless he made this known by means of a derogatory clause.[38]

Castropalao felt that it was more probably correct to hold that a second granted privilege, if it was a special or a particular one, was valid notwithstanding all lack of mention of any contrary general privilege. He referred to a Rule of Boniface VIII, which stated that a genus is derogated by its species;[39] and this was especially true when the species in point of time followed the genus. Castropalao also stated that the second privilege, if it was a particular one, was not directly contrary to the first general privilege, but simply an exception to it.[40]

Suarez came to the conclusion that a particular privilege would be valid even though an existing general privilege contravened such a privilege. He quoted the same rule of Boniface VIII, that a genus is derogated by its species, even though no mention of the previously existing general privilege was made in the special privilege. His reason was that the superior in granting the general privilege did not neutralize his own power to give some special privilege, even though this was contrary to or in some way

---

[36] C. 1, *de constitutionibus,* I, 2, in VI°

[37] Suarez, *ibid.,* n. 6, p. 413.

[38] Castropalao, *ibid.,* § 13.

[39] Reg. 34, R. J., in VI°.

[40] Castropalao, *ibid.,* § 14.

opposed to the general privilege. But even if it was contrary, it could hardly be said to be contrary in the proper sense of the word, since it rather evinced an exception to the general law.[41]

The third method, according to Castropalao, by means of which a previous privilege was revoked, even apart from all legislation, was through the passing of a sentence or judgment contrary to the prior privilege. This was true as long as the one passing the sentence had also the power to revoke the privilege. Castropalao vindicated the applicability of this method in the following manner: a judicial sentence has the same effect as a law; but a law can revoke a privilege; therefore, a judicial sentence can also revoke a privilege. It was postulated, of course, that the sentence be a just one, and passed by the superior with a knowledge of the existence of the previous privilege.

Likewise, a sentence also revoked a privilege when the privileged person was deprived of his privilege in punishment for a crime he had committed. This, then, was not simply a tacit, but rather an express, revocation. But the sentence revoking the privilege had to be given by the one who granted the privilege or with the latter's permission, since an inferior could not deprive subjects of privileges that had been granted to them by someone superior to both of them.[42]

ARTICLE 5. NECESSITY OF THE PROMULGATION OF THE REVOCATION OF A PRIVILEGE

Castropalao taught that if a revocation was to be effected by law, then the law had to be published or promulgated. Promulgation was for law a necessary quality. If a civil law was revoked and this revocation was to have effect in the whole country, then a two months' period had to elapse before the revocation took effect. If the revocation was meant for only one province, then it took effect after there had elapsed a sufficient time for the people to learn of the revocation. Castropalao felt that in regard to ecclesiastical laws, as long as the revocation had been published in

---

[41] Suarez, *De Legibus,* lib. VIII, cap. 39, n 7,—*Opera Omnia,* VI, p. 414.
[42] Castropalao, I, tr. 3, disp. 4, p. 21, n. 4, § 17.

Rome, that sufficed for the revocation of an ecclesiastical privilege contained in those laws.[43]

Suarez held that a single publication in the city of the superior sufficed, and that it was not necessary to make a new publication of the revocation in every diocese. Suarez indicated that when the revocation of the privilege of entering the convents of nuns was made, this revocation was promulgated only in Rome.[44]

But according to just and right reason the revocation of a privilege should not have its effect until the people had at least gained all knowledge of it, even though in acting against an unknown revocation they of course remained without guilt. If the revocation would have taken effect immediately upon promulgation, then the natural order of things would have been needlessly disturbed.[45]

In referring to private revocations, Suarez contended that the privileged person did not lose his privilege until he had received special notice of the revocation. This followed from the very nature of a private revocation. Therefore an effective notice had to be served to the individual person. However, Suarez did not insist that this had to be effected by means of a personal letter or a special messenger. As long as the one who revoked the privilege used adequate means to make his will known to the possessor of the privilege, the revocation gained effect. It was not necessary that the privileged person was willing and ready to accept the revocation of the privilege. It sufficed if he simply knew about it.[46]

---

[43] *Ibid.*, n. 5, § 1.

[44] Suarez, *De Legibus*, lib. VIII, cap. 40, n. 1,—*Opera Omnia*, VI, p. 414.

[45] Suarez, *ibid.*, n. 3, p. 415.

[46] Suarez, *ibid.*, n. 6, p. 416.

SECTION II

Revocation of Privileges According to Reiffenstuel and Schmalzgrueber

ARTICLE 1. WHAT PRIVILEGES COULD BE REVOKED?

Schmalzgrueber (1663-1735) taught that, if privileges had been granted to persons who were not subjects of the grantor, and if these privileges had been accepted, then the grantor could not revoke these privileges except for the public good.[47]

The reason for this, he said, was that the privilege, once it had been granted to such persons, became theirs, so that they had a real right to it. It could not be taken from them except for the public good. It would have affected the public good if the privilege had been used to the detriment of the country of the grantor, or to the detriment of the grantor himself, and therefore as a result the use of it would have been unjust and wicked. In those cases the grantor of the privilege, his successor, and also his superior could revoke the privilege.

Suarez, Castropalao, and Reiffenstuel (1642-1703) all held the same opinion with regard to that situation.[48] They taught that a privilege of this kind contained the condition that, if it became an evil or an unjust privilege, then it would cease by itself, even if the grantor did not revoke it.

Therefore, the privileges usually revoked were those that had been given to the subjects of the one granting the privilege. And among these privileges the one that could be revoked with the least amount of difficulty was the generous privilege, which some commentators classified in the same category with a gift. In this,

---

[47] *Ius Ecclesiasticum Universum* (5 vols. in 12, Romae, 1843-1845), lib. V, tit. 33, n. 219 (hereafter cited as Schmalzgrueber).

[48] Suarez, *De Legibus,* lib. VIII, cap. 37, n. 2,—*Opera Omnia,* VI, p. 405; Castropalao, I, tr. 3, disp. 4, p. 21, n. 1; Reiffenstuel, *Ius Canonicum Universum iuxta titulos quinque librorum decretalium* (5 vols. in 6, Romae, 1831-1834), lib. V, tit. 33, n. 121 (hereafter cited as Reiffenstuel).

however, Reiffenstuel did not agree with them. He pointed out an essential difference. A gift, he said, becomes the property of the one to whom it is given, and it cannot be taken back without the donor's showing his complete ingratitude and bad manners. But the right or favor given by means of a generous privilege does not pass into the ownership (*dominium*) of the privileged person as does a gift, but rather it always remains dependent on the will of the one granting it, and in consequence can be revoked validly by him even without a reason, although this would not be the proper thing for a superior to do.[49]

ARTICLE 2. REVOCATION OF GENEROUS AND REMUNERATIVE PRIVILEGES

A remunerative privilege, according to Schmalzgrueber, is a privilege given as a reward for meritorious work done either by the privileged person himself, or by his parents or relatives, or it is a privilege given to an Order or a Society for meritorious work done by its members. A generous privilege is a privilege which is given out of the generosity of the grantor, and not in consideration of merit on the part of the one receiving the privilege.

Schmalzgrueber stated that a superior could revoke a generous privilege which he had given to one of his subjects, since the subject never gained the ownership (*dominium*) of the generous privilege. However, he was of the same opinion with Reiffenstuel, who held that the generous privilege should not be revoked without a reason, since it was fitting that a favor given by a superior should be of a permanent nature.[50]

A remunerative privilege given out of justice could not be revoked. A remunerative privilege given out of gratitude was not as irrevocable as the one given out of justice, but it remained irrevocable until a sufficient compensation was made. Schmalzgrueber agreed with Suarez and Castropalao in saying that the privilege given by means of a contract could not be revoked without a just cause. This seemed evident, since the privilege was

---

[49] Reiffenstuel, *ibid.*, n. 120.

[50] Schmalzgrueber, *ibid.*, n. 221; Reiffenstuel, *loc. cit.*

obtained by means of a contract, and, inasmuch as both parties were bound by the contract, it would have contravened justice to break the contract without a just cause.[51]

Reiffenstuel called the remunerative privilege a pact entered into by the superior and by the subject in consideration of work already done, and therefore it was not in the same category as a generous privilege. Accordingly a grave cause affecting the common good had to be present before the privilege could be revoked.[52]

ARTICLE 3. WHO COULD REVOKE PRIVILEGES?

In discussing the persons who could revoke privileges that were freely granted to a subject, Schmalzgrueber taught that the one who granted the privilege, whether it was the Holy Father or some subordinate prelate, could revoke the privilege. This rule suffered an exception when the privilege had been granted by a lower prelate, but later had been confirmed by a higher prelate. By reason of the confirmation the privilege depended on the will of the one who had confirmed it, and without his consent it could not be revoked. Likewise, if a subordinate had received the power to dispense from the law of a superior, he was under the necessity of acting according to the will of the superior when he dispensed. To revoke the privilege and to restore the obligation of the law dispensed from, he needed the consent of the superior, since that revocation exceeded the ordinary power he had in the matter. He had indeed been given power to dispense from the law, but not to re-impose the law by revoking some privilege he has previously granted.[53]

Not only the one granting the privilege but also his successor had the power to revoke privileges. This was so because he succeeded in equal power. According to a fiction of law he constituted with the predecessor one and the same person. The predecessor could not bind the hand of his successor any more than he could bind his own. Also a privilege granted by a subordinate could be revoked by his superior. There had to exist some reason for doing

---

[51] Schmalzgrueber, *ibid.*, n. 224.

[52] Reiffenstuel, *ibid.*, n. 122.

[53] Schmalzgrueber, *ibid.*, n. 227.

this, and unless a reason was present even the supreme legislator would revoke the privilege illicitly, since such a revocation would be harmful to the subordinate prelate and detrimental to his subjects. Any other higher prelate in the absence of a just reason would probably revoke the privilege invalidly, since he could not take away the rights of his subjects unjustly, and in this case the subordinate prelate would have certain rights over those privileges which he himself gave out.[54]

ARTICLE 4. DIFFERENT MEANS BY WHICH PRIVILEGES WERE REVOKED

Schmalzgrueber and Reiffenstuel indicated two ways for the revocation of privileges: tacit and express revocation. Express revocation could be effected not only by means of a special revocation but also by means of a general revocation, except in the three cases which had been singled out by Suarez and Castropalao.[55] The three exceptions involved: 1) those privileges which were enacted in the main part of a law; 2) those privileges which called for a special mention before being revoked; and 3) those privileges which had been obtained in the manner of a contract. Schmalzgrueber added that even in these three exceptional cases the granted privilege could be revoked by way of a general revocation if it was understood that the exceptional cases were also included in the revocation.[56]

Tacit revocation was effected by the superior when he placed an act which was directly contrary to the privilege and which could not have its intended effect apart from the revocation of the privilege. However, for the gaining of this effect it was necessary that there be warrant for the presumption that the superior knew of the existence of the earlier privilege and also that he had the intention of revoking it, since the revocation postulated a free and a voluntary act. This freedom and voluntariness could hardly accompany this act unless the person in his act of revocation had some knowledge of the existing privilege. Reiffenstuel

---

[54] Schmalzgrueber, *ibid.*, nn. 228-229.

[55] Suarez, *De Legibus*, lib. VIII, cap. 38, n. 1,—*Opera Omnia*, VI, p. 410; Castropalao, I, tr. 3, dist. 4, p. 21, n. 4.

[56] Schmalzgrueber, *ibid.*, n. 229; Reiffenstuel, *ibid.*, n. 124.

furnished an example of an action that tacitly revoked a privilege. For instance, when a universal law is enacted, even though it does not expressly revoke any privileges, it is considered as revoking the privileges mentioned in the universal law that is being abrogated, since the one who is enacting the new law is presumed to know of the impart of the earlier law, and of the privileges mentioned therein.[57]

But a prior private privilege was not revoked by a later contrary one, even tacitly, unless special mention was made of the prior privilege. The superior was considered not to know of the private privilege when he did not make any mention of it, and therefore the second privilege did not abrogate the first. The two exceptions to this rule were the cases in which the superior could not be presumed ignorant, with reference namely to the prior privileges that existed in the universal law, and with reference also to the general privilege giving way to the later special privilege.[58]

ARTICLE 5. WHAT PRIVILEGES OF REGULARS WERE REVOKED BY THE COUNCIL OF TRENT?

It is certain that many of the privileges of regulars were not revoked by the Council of Trent. They still exist, and some were even confirmed by the Council of Trent. It is certain also that all those privileges which were contrary to the decrees of the twenty-fifth session of the Council were revoked, and no longer continued to exist, unless they were granted since the time of the Council and as contrary to the Tridentine decrees which forbade such privileges.[59]

Reiffenstuel pointed out that some decrees of the Council of Trent added a clause revoking contrary privileges, and others abstracted from the use of such a clause. It seems that this clause would have been added in vain if every decree was to be considered as revoking contrary privileges even when a revoking clause was not added. Therefore those privileges which were contrary to a

[57] Reiffenstuel, *ibid.*, nn. 128-129.

[58] *Ibid.*, n. 130.

[59] Schmalzgrueber, *ibid.*, n. 234.

decree of the Council of Trent, but not contrary to any decree revoking all contrary privileges, continued in valid effect.[60]

ARTICLE 6. WHEN DID THE REVOCATION OF A PRIVILEGE HAVE ITS EFFECT?

A revocation had its effect on a privilege when the revocation had been sufficiently promulgated. If it was a revocation through a contrary law, then promulgation in the curia or in the place for which the law was made could prove sufficient. The revocation did not take effect immediately; it took effect only after a certain period, which in civil law was two months in the time of the Roman Empire. In Canon Law the time was of a shorter or a longer duration depending on the nature of the privilege. The revocation became binding at the time indicated for it, even if some of the people were still ignorant of the revocation, or of the new law, or of the privilege that revoked a previous privilege, since, as Reiffenstuel had stated, "in law, that which is common to all is taken as the norm, and not that which is rare or accidental."[61]

When a revocation was made *ab homine,* that is, by an individual person or personally, then the revocation did not have its effect until the person enjoying the privilege was directly notified. There was excluded, then, any and every casual revocation. It was in the interests of proper government that the superior should want the privileged person to use his privileges until the latter knew that they had been revoked. In any assumption to the contrary the superior would have occasioned many invalid acts. Since the privileged person was given a special notice by letter or rescript or by some similar means at the time when the privilege was granted to him, it was proper that he should also be given a special notice at the time when the privilege was being revoked.[62]

---

[60] Reiffenstuel, *ibid.,* n. 139.

[61] *Ibid.,* n. 133.

[62] Schmalzgrueber, *ibid.,* n. 245.

PART TWO

Canonical Commentary

CHAPTER III

Loss of Privileges by Revocation

Canon 71. *Per legem generalem revocantur privilegia in hoc Codice contenta; ad cetera quod attinct servetur praescriptum can. 60.*

Privileges contained in the Code are revoked by a general contrary law; with respect to other privileges canon 67 is to be observed.[1]

ARTICLE 1. TACIT REVOCATION OF PRIVILEGES

From the pages of history it is made quite clear that the Apostolic See adopted from Roman Law the notion of privileges and made this a part of its own legislation. This adoption of the notion of privileges started many centuries before Gratian published his momentous work, but the doctrinal explanation of privileges awaited his masterful exposition. Augustine (1872-1943) stated in his commentary on the Code that in a famous *dictum* Gratian solved the objection raised by the asserted necessity of a strict observance of the canons of the councils and of the decrees of the popes as follows: The Roman Church has the authority to establish laws, but it is not bound by them, because it is the head and support of all the churches, and all the laws have attached to them the implicit clause, "*salvo iure sanctae Romanae Ecclesiae.*" Hence if privileges are granted which apparently are against the universal law, they do not clash with the right of the Church, because all privileges are reserved to it. From this point of view it followed that no privileges are granted except for the honor and utility of the Church, and that privileges are revocable.[2]

---

[1] English translation of Canon 71 is taken from Amleto Giovanni Cicognani, *Canon Law* (2. ed. revised, Westminster, Md.: The Newman Press, 1949), 806 (hereafter cited as Cicognani).

[2] Augustine, *A Commentary on the New Code of Canon Law* (8 vols., Vol. I, 4. ed., St. Louis, Herder, 1921), I, 152 (hereafter cited as Augustine).

There can be no doubt today that the Church has continued with and developed these principles of Gratian concerning privileges and their revocation, and there is evidence of this in the present Code of Canon Law. In the first part of canon 71 it is stated that privileges contained in the Code are revoked by means of a general law, and the second part of the canon states that with respect to other privileges canon 60 is to be observed. This second part of the canon means that all those privileges which are not mentioned in the Code are revoked according to the rules for the revocation of rescripts.

A revocation of a privilege is an act by which a legitimate superior takes away for the future some privilege which had previously been granted. This can be done either tacitly and indirectly, or expressly by means of a direct revocation. The indirect or tacit revocation will be considered first.

In the tacit revocation a superior knowingly places an action which hinders some privilege from having its desired effect. With reference to the privileges mentioned in the Code, a general or a universal law will tacitly revoke these privileges if the general or universal law concerns itself with the same material that is found in the privilege, and it is impossible for the privilege and the new universal law to be harmonized. Van Hove (1872-1947) stated that a general, i.e., universal, law must be understood as a law that has been given for the whole Latin Church, and not simply as a law that applies in a larger territory as compared with one that applies in a smaller territory.[8]

As a parallel case the same principle that is found in canon 22 concerning the cessation of laws would have application here. Canon 22 states that a later law, when given by a competent authority, abrogates an earlier one if it expressly says so, or if it is directly contrary to it, or if it reorders the subject matter of the older law; however canon 6, number 1, of this Code remains in full force, that is to say, a general law in no wise derogates

[8] *Commentarium Lovaniense in Codicem Iuris Canonici,* Vol. I (5 tomes, Mechliniae-Romae: H. Dessain, 1928-1939), Tomus V, *De Privilegiis—De Dispensationibus,* p. 206 (hereafter cited as *De Privilegiis*).

from the laws in force in particular places or with regard to particular persons unless the contrary is expressly provided therein.[4]

1. *Tacit Revocation of Privileges Mentioned in the Code*

It is required, therefore, that the general or universal law, when it revokes a privilege mentioned in the Code, be directly contrary to the privilege recounted in the Code. It must treat of the same matter, in the same degree and extent, and must also apply to the same group of people to whom the privilege was given, since there can be, for instance, a universal law which applies only to the clergy, or there may be a universal law which will apply only to the laity.

Cicognani says that privileges recounted in the Code are general privileges, and that they exist after the fashion of general laws. Consequently in order to revoke privileges recounted in the Code a new general law must be enacted and promulgated which will later be inserted in the Code according to the norm of the Motu Proprio *Cum Iuris Canonici* of September 15, 1917.[5]

When a doubt arises on whether or not some new universal law completely abrogates a privilege recounted in the Code, certain principles which can be drawn from the Code ought to be considered. First of all, according to canon 70 a privilege must be regarded as a permanent one unless the contrary is evident. Although this refers to a privilege considered in itself, the same principle seems to apply when there is doubt concerning its revocation. The privilege will remain, therefore, unless the contrary is evident.

The second principle to be considered is that which arises in a case parallel to the revocation of privileges, and that is the revocation of a law. Canon 23 states that when there is doubt whether or not a law has been revoked, it may not be presumed that the law has been revoked, but the new law should be adapted to the old, and both made to harmonize, as far as possible.[6]

---

[4] Can. 22.

[5] Cicognani, p. 807.

[6] Can. 23.

Therefore with the application of this same principle to privileges when there is a doubt concerning their revocation, a privilege may not be presumed to be revoked, but must be examined carefully in its relation to the new general law, before one can see whether or not there is a complete revocation, a partial revocation, or whether there is perhaps no revocation at all, inasmuch as the new general law and the privilege can be harmonized, so that there results no revocation of the privilege.

2. *Tacit Revocation of Privileges Not Mentioned in the Code*

In the second part of canon 71 it is stated that the revocation of privileges which are not mentioned in the Code is governed by the legislation found in canon 60.[7] Canon 60 deals with the revocation of rescripts and reads as follows:

> If a rescript is revoked by a special act of the superior, it is valid until the one who obtained the rescript is notified of the revocation. Rescripts are not revoked by a contrary law unless the law expressly so provides or unless it has been granted by an authority superior to the one who issued the rescript.[8]

The first part of canon 60 deals with the express and direct revocation of a rescript. The second part of canon 60 adverts to a direct or explicit revocation of rescripts which is effected by means of a contrary law containing an express revocation or a derogatory clause that accomplishes the revocation. Also treated in the second part of canon 60 is the tacit revocation of rescripts. This tacit revocation of rescripts occurs when the superior of the one who granted a rescript issues a law contrary to what is contained in the rescript. No explicit revocation need be mentioned, for the reason that the superior is presumed not to know of the existence of particular privileges and consequently omits all mention of them. Furthermore, no subordinate legislator is empowered to act contrary to the commands of his superior.[9]

---

[7] Can. 71.

[8] English translation of canon 60 is taken from Cicognani, p. 770.

[9] Cicognani, p. 808.

The second part of canon 71 mentions that with respect to other privileges, that is, such as are not mentioned in the Code, canon 60 is to be observed.[10] Abbo-Hannan point out that all privileges granted through the universal law were at the time of its promulgation restricted to those which are mentioned in the Code; if mention of them was omitted, they were to be considered as suppressed. On the other hand, new privileges granted through the universal law after the promulgation of the Code are to be inserted in it.[11]

Therefore in canon 60 the law on the revocation of rescripts is applied literally, as canon 71 prescribes, to the revocation of particular privileges which exist outside the Code of Canon Law.

Since canon 60 is taken literally as regards the revocation of particular privileges, the word "privilege" may be supplied wherever the word "rescript" is found in the canon. Thus the second paragraph of canon 60 would read: a privilege is not revoked by means of a contrary law unless the law expressly so provides, or unless it has been granted by an authority superior to the one who issued the privilege.

A particular or universal law, therefore, even though it were entirely contrary to some particular privilege, would not revoke that privilege unless the law expressly so provided, or unless the law was enacted by the superior of the one who gave the privilege. The same principle is found in the first paragraph of canon 48, which states that, if it should happen that two rescripts referring to the same matter are contradictory, the rescript containing a peculiar or particular enactment must be accepted in preference to the one containing a general enactment. And in the second paragraph it is stated that, if both rescripts alike are particular or general, the one which is dated or received earlier must be preferred to that of a later date, unless specific mention is made in the latter rescript of the earlier one.[12]

---

[10] Can. 71.

[11] Abbo-Hannan, *The Sacred Canons* (2 vols., St. Louis, London: B. Herder Book Co., 1952), I, 70 (hereafter cited as Abbo-Hannan).

[12] Can. 48.

Therefore, a universal or a particular law issued by the Roman Pontiff would not abrogate a particular pontifical privilege, though the former were entirely contrary to the latter, unless the Roman Pontiff expressly provided for this in the law just issued by expressly revoking contrary privileges by name, or by adding to the law a derogatory clause that will effectively revoke all contrary privileges. Herein the doctrine of canon 60 differs from that of canon 22, which treats of laws. Canon 22 declares that a more recent law abolishes a former law, if the new law is directly contrary to it. And rightly so, since a rescript assumes a special character.[13]

When a privilege is revoked by means of a contrary law, this must be expressly provided for in the law itself by way of mention of the revocation of certain privileges, or by way of added clauses in the law that would have the effect of abrogating those privileges. Such clauses as "*non obstantibus privilegiis,*" or "*revocatis quibuscunque privilegiis,*" would revoke generous privileges, according to Beste,[14] but not remunerative privileges, nor those obtained by way of a contract. He says that such a clause as, "*non obstantibus quibuscunque privilegiis, etiamsi expressa et specifica mentione dignis,*" or "*sub quacunque verborum forma conceptis,*" would revoke the remunerative privileges. The onerous privileges or those given in the form of a contract, or found in concordats, will usually be revoked when the words "*etiamsi per modum contractus concessa*" have been added to the derogatory clause of a contrary law.

ARTICLE 2. EXPRESS REVOCATION OF PRIVILEGES

The meaning of express revocation is so obvious from the words themselves that its definition is somewhat of a redundancy. Wernz (1842-1914) stated that the express revocation of a privilege is had if a certain privilege is named specifically as recalled or abrogated; or, again, a privilege is revoked expressly when a

---

[13] Cicognani, p. 770.

[14] *Introductio in Codicem* (Collegeville, Minn.: St. John's Abbey Press, 1948), p. 122 (hereafter cited as Beste).

general clause with the necessary emplitude and efficacy has been attached to a new law or privilege.[15]

This express revocation can be effected by either the legislator himself, by his successor, or by his superior. It will be valid for all kinds of privileges, whether they be generous privileges, remunerative, onerous, or conventional. For the revocation of a generous privilege a just cause is required. For the revocation of a remunerative privilege a graver cause is required than that which suffices for the revocation of a generous privilege. And for the valid revocation of a privilege that has become a real pact, it is the public good, that must demand its revocation.

The Code's legislation for express revocation is contained in the first part of canon 60. It states that if a rescript is revoked by means of a special act of the superior it is valid until the one who obtained the rescript is notified of the revocation.[16] Therefore in the case of privileges not mentioned in the Code, their express revocation will not take effect until the one who obtained the privilege or the one who enjoys the privilege is notified by his superior of the privilege's revocation. This applies especially in those cases wherein an individual person or a particular community is being deprived of some privilege. According to Cicognani, the first part of canon 60 refers to a particular rescript, since a general rescript is equivalent to a law, and therefore requires a public revocation.[17] Applied to privileges this means that, if a general privilege is being revoked, then a public revocation similar to that of a law must be made and every individual will be presumed to have heard of its revocation. However, if a particular privilege is revoked, then its effect will not take place until the person who enjoys the privilege is notified of its revocation.

ARTICLE 3. REASONS FOR THE REVOCATION OF PRIVILEGES

The common opinion of the decretists and decretalists was that a reason was required before a revocation could take place.[18]

---

[15] *Ius Decretalium* (6 vols., Vol. 1, 2. ed., Romae, 1905), I, 205.

[16] Can. 60, § 1.

[17] Cicognani, p. 770.

[18] Van Hove, *De Privilegiis*, p. 216.

Hostiensis (+ 1271) taught that this cause or reason was required, not indeed for validity, but of course for lawfulness, since it would not be fitting for a superior to revoke a privilege without a reason for doing so, since the revocation would be ascribed to his inconsistency or levity.[19] Likewise a privilege granted to the Church by the head of some government with the approval of the Holy See could not be revoked without the permission of the Holy See. In like manner a privilege granted by a subordinate could not be revoked by the same subordinate once it has been confirmed by his superior, since the confirmation makes it part of the superior's legislation.

The revocation of a generous privilege is valid and licit as long as there is present a legitimate reason. This follows from the fact that the privilege is still within the power of the one who granted it, and also from the fact that the person who granted it did not give up his right to revoke the privilege if the occasion or a legitimate reason demanded it. The granting of a generous privilege depends upon the will of the grantor exclusively, and its revocation will likewise rest solely with him.

A problem does arise whenever a right has been acquired or there has been a transfer of ownership (*dominium*) in relation to some privilege. Such a privilege then would be governed not only by the laws of privileges but also by the laws of contracts. A revocation of such a privilege would be valid only if the obligations of justice have been observed.

This is particularly true in those cases in which a privilege has been granted to a non-subject. It is true that the grantor can retain his right to recall the privilege whenever he feels he has a just reason to do so, but in most of these cases the privilege is given after the manner of a contract, if not a formal one at least a tacit one, and the laws that govern the revocation of contracts must be observed. Therefore only when the recipient of the privilege has broken the contract should the grantor of the privilege revoke the privilege.[20]

---

[19] Hostiensis, lib. V, tit. 33, n. 10.

[20] Gommarus Michiels, *Normae Generales Iuris Canonici, Commentarius Libri I Codicis Iuris Canonici* (2. ed., 2 vols., Tornaci: Desclee et Socii, 1949), II, 597-598 (hereafter cited as Michiels).

The legislator who grants a privilege can grant it with the understood condition that the privilege will be revoked whenever its use may become detrimental to the common good. Therefore whenever, through a change of circumstances, the privilege has become harmful, either to the one for whom it was granted or to the common good, a declaration shall be made that the privilege was not extended to such circumstances, and therefore it is now revoked.[21]

As regards the privileges that have been granted to those who are subjects of the grantor of the privileges a distinction must be made. When a privilege has been given under the title of a generous privilege it must be understood that this privilege depends for its continued existence on the will of the grantor, so that the subject does not have a real right to it. It therefore will cease to exist when the grantor has changed his mind concerning the privilege, and has made known its revocation.

A subject who has obtained a privilege in the form of a contract cannot have his privilege revoked unless the common good or the public utility demands the revocation. In this case there is usually demanded some compensation in connection with the breaking of the contract, since the lawgiver does not have absolute dominion over the goods of his subject.[22]

Likewise a subject who has obtained a remunerative privilege may lose it by way of revocation if its continued use would militate against the public good. If the remunerative privilege was given out of justice, then there must be a compensation for the loss of the privilege. If the remunerative privilege was given out of mere gratitude, then the reason for revoking it must be more serious than the reason demanded for the revocation of a generous privilege, but there would not be the same obligation to give any compensation for the loss of this privilege as there would be for one given out of justice.

---

[21] Van Hove, *De Privilegiis,* p. 217.

[22] *Ibid.,* p. 220.

ARTICLE 4. CERTAIN PRIVILEGES REVOKED BY THE SACRED PENITENTIARY

On March 20, 1933, the Sacred Penitentiary issued the decree *Consilium suum,*[23] which revoked as of April 1, 1933, which was the date of publication of the respective fascicle of the *Acta Apostolicae Sedis,* many privileges and faculties which dealt with indulgences. It revoked all those concessions which had been made to any pious association of whatsoever name or nature, and in virtue of which priest members were empowered to bless religious articles and to attach to them the Apostolic or Brigittine indulgences, to enrich rosaries with the respective indulgences, to attach to crucifixes either the indulgences of the Way of the Cross in favor of those legitimately hindered from making the Stations, or the plenary indulgence for the hour of death, or to bestow the papal blessing at the end of sermons, or were granted the indult of a personal privileged altar.

There was a good deal of misunderstanding concerning the decree *Consilium suum,* especially regarding the ones who were affected by the decree. *The Ecclesiastical Review* for June, 1933, interpreted the decree to mean that all the priests who had the use of certain privileges or faculties in virtue of membership in any confraternity, pious union, pious association and the like, lost those privileges if those privileges were listed amongst the privileges enumerated in the decree and revoked by the decree. The *Review* went on to say that if those same priests enjoyed those privileges or faculties by virtue of a personal indult or some similar source, then they would still retain them.[24]

The decree itself said that if in the future priests desire any of the above mentioned faculties they must present to the Sacred Penitentiary a request duly recommended by their ordinary or superior. It also reminded everyone that the decree in no way

---

[23] *Acta Apostolicae Sedis, Commentarium Officiale* (Romae, 1909-1929; Civitate Vaticana, 1929—), XXV (1933), 170-171 (hereafter cited as *AAS*).

[24] Studies and Conferences: "Revocation of Certain Faculties and Indults concerning Indulgences"—*The American Ecclesiastical Review* (Vols. I-XXXII, Philadelphia, 1889-1905; *The Ecclesiastical Review,* Philadelphia, 1905-1943; from 1944, *The American Ecclesiastical Review,* Washington, D. C., Vol. CX, 1944-), LXXXVII (1933), 621-622.

touched the privileges enjoyed by certain religious Orders and Congregations, namely of blessing and enriching rosaries with certain indulgences, or crucifixes with the indulgence of the Way of the Cross for the benefit of those who are hindered from making the Stations, or also of erecting the Way of the Cross. And, finally, it forbade the superiors of such communities to give out these faculties and privileges to any but members of their own institute.

The decree however did not revoke the privileges of those priests who had already obtained them. It revoked the future granting of those privileges by the associations referred to in the decree, but it did not disturb the possession of those who had obtained them before the date of the promulgation of the decree, which was April 1, 1933. The *Acta Apostolicae Sedis* of 1937 contain a response of the Sacred Penitentiary to some doubts that had arisen regarding the revocation enacted in the decree *Consilium suum*. The first question was whether or not clerics who were not ordained to the priesthood but who had become members of the associations mentioned in the decree before April 1, 1933, enjoyed the privileges of those associations. The answer was in the negative. The second question asked whether or not those priests who were members of the association before April 1, 1933, but who had not yet been approved for the hearing of confessions at that time, could enjoy the faculties and privileges of the association? The answer was in the affirmative, but it forbade the use of those privileges and faculties which entitled a priest to give the Apostolic and Plenary Indulgence *in articulo mortis* until the priest had received the faculties to hear confessions.[25]

Another and very obvious conclusion that could be drawn from the answers the Sacred Penitentiary has given is that all the priests who were members of the mentioned association before April 1, 1933, and had faculties to hear confessions, did not lose any of the privileges or faculties recounted in the decree. The decree therefore revoked the future granting of those privileges by the associations mentioned, and also revoked the use of them by those few clerics who had already obtained the privileges but had not yet

[25] *AAS,* XXIX (1937), 58.

received the Sacred Order of Priesthood, and restricted the use of some of the privileges by those priests who were not yet approved for the hearing of confessions.

Was the element of remuneration indicated as present in any of the cases mentioned above when the revocation of the Sacred Penitentiary took effect? The essential thing that must be decided is whether these were generous privileges or remunerative privileges. A generous privilege derives through the liberality of the grantor in acknowledged abstraction from the previous merit of the recipient. A remunerative privilege is granted in view of some special merit, for the rewarding of merit, or in gratitude for some particular service.[26]

If the privileges were given as generous privileges, then there would be no need of any compensation either on the part of the Holy See, or on the part of the pious associations, when the privileges were revoked by the Sacred Penitentiary. However, if the privileges were remunerative or onerous privileges, then in justice some remuneration or compensation should have been given to those who were deprived of them. The pious associations themselves most probably received their privileges by way of generosity from the Holy See upon a submitted petition. If the Holy See revokes such privileges, no compensation is demanded. Those who enrolled in the pious associations previous to the revocation of April 1, 1933, and lost their right to the privileges and faculties because of the revocation, deserved some kind of compensation. This could have consisted in the returning of their enrollment fee, since those who enrolled in those pious associations did so mostly out of consideration of the privileges and faculties they were to receive by being members of said pious associations.

ARTICLE 5. CANON 613, § 1, AND CANON 4 IN RELATION TO THE REVOCATION OF PRIVILEGES

1. *Canon 613, § 1*

Shortly after the promulgation of the new Code a great controversy arose regarding the question whether or not all the priv-

[26] Cicognani, p. 782.

ileges gained by religious through an associated participation were revoked by the law enacted in canon 613, § 1. Canon 613, § 1, states that each religious institute enjoys only those privileges which are mentioned in the Code or which may have been granted to it directly by the Holy See; every associated sharing of privileges for the future is revoked.[27] An article that appeared in the *Apollinaris* in 1932 by Honestus Tatjer cited the opinions of 73 commentators concerning the meaning of canon 613, § 1. Forty of these authors held the more common opinion that canon 613, § 1, should be understood in the sense that with reference to the future there could no longer be any sharing of privileges among religious, but that the privileges which they had obtained in that manner previous to the new Code they were permitted to retain and use; nineteen commentators felt that canon 613, § 1, revoked all the privileges obtained in the past by means of an associated sharing with others, as it also revoked for the future this means of obtaining privileges; fourteen commentators felt that the meaning of the law was not clear from the way the law was written in the Code.[28]

The word "only" in canon 613, § 1, could seem to limit the privileges of religious institutes to the privileges mentioned in the Code and to the privileges granted directly to the religious institute by way of a concession from the Holy See. Accordingly there could seem to be revoked or abrogated all other privileges which any religious institute enjoyed up to the time of the Code. The expression "privileges contained in the Code" points to the privileges enumerated in the Code or confirmed by the Code. "Privileges which may have been directly conceded to it by the Apostolic See," namely, the privileges granted directly to a religious institute before the Code, are governed by canon 4 of the Code, which states that acquired rights and likewise privileges and indults previously granted by the Apostolic See to persons either physical or moral, as long as they were still in

---

[27] Can. 613, § 1.

[28] *Apollinaris* (Romae, 1928-   ), V (1932), 458-486.

use and not revoked, remain in their entirety, unless they are expressly revoked in the canons of the Code.[29]

The expression "for the future" in the concluding clause of canon 613, § 1, renders the meaning of the preceding words somewhat uncertain, and there were canonists such as Biederlack (+ 1930), Blat (+ 1943), Bondini (+ 1936), Ferreres (+ 1936), Leitner (+ 1929), Santamaria and others who held that all privileges obtained by way of associated participation were lost. Others, such as Augustine (+ 1943), Badii (+ 1938), Cocchi, Creusen, Fanfani (+ 1955), Noval (+ 1938), Prümmer (+ 1931), and Vermeersch (+ 1936) held that for the future there could no more be any sharing in privileges among religious institutes, but that all privileges acquired in this manner throughout the past could still be utilized.

This latter opinion seemed to express the intention of the legislator, and was also in agreement with the principles found in the new Code, especially in canons 4, 10 and 19. Canon 4 stated that privileges which had not been recalled and were still in use remained as they were unless they were expressly revoked in the canons of the Code.[30]

Canon 10 states that laws affect the future and not the past, unless it is expressly stated therein that they are retroactive; and canon 29 states that custom is the best interpreter of laws. Therefore if the religious have had a privilege for one hundred years or from time immemorial and it has not been expressly revoked by the present Code, then the privilege will remain and canon 613, § 1, will revoke only for the future the potential obtaining of privileges through an associated participation. The question was settled by the Code Commission in a reply given on December 30, 1937. The answer was in the negative to the question whether the words of canon 613, § 1, *"exclusa in posterum qualibet communicatione,"* are to be understood in the sense that privileges which were acquired through an associated participation and peacefully enjoyed by religious institutes before the Code of Canon Law were revoked.[31]

---

[29] Can. 4.

[30] Can. 4.

[31] *AAS,* XXX (1938), 73.

2. *Canon 4*

Canon 4 states that acquired rights and likewise privileges and indults granted up to that time by the Apostolic See to persons, either physical or moral, remain in their entirely, if they are still in use and not recalled, unless they are expressly revoked by the canons of the Code. Canon 4 does not take into consideration the privileges granted by ordinaries intermediate to the Roman Pontiff. Many of these may have been lost in consequence of the ruling in canon 60, § 2, which indicates that rescripts are revoked by way of a contrary law if the law has been issued by an authority superior to the one who granted the rescript.[32] Therefore the privileges mentioned in rescripts given by an authority inferior to the Holy See are lost whenever a contrary law has been issued by an authority superior to the one who granted the rescript.

Canon 6, n. 1, abrogates particular legislation opposed to the Code. If a privilege is mentioned in some particular legislation contrary to the Code, it also will cease to exist by virtue of canon 6, n. 1. However, it is not always easy to determine whether a special concession made to some particular locality was in reality a true law or simply a privilege. If it was a contrary law, then it becomes abrogated through canon 6; if it was a privilege, then it will not become abrogated through canon 6; if it was a privilege, then it will become abrogated only when some other express revocation is found in the Code.

For the retention of previously granted privileges canon 4 postulates that the privileges must have actually been in use at the time the Code was enacted. Hence those privileges which were revoked previous to the Code are not revived by canon 4, and moreover the Code by means of an abrogating clause could and did revoke privileges that were in existence up to the time of the Code. The Index of the Code lists a number of the privileges which the Code itself has revoked. The following are some of the privileges revoked:

1) Canon 343, § 2, revoked the privilege or custom that restricted the bishop's choice concerning the two members of the clergy who

---

[32] Can. 60.

were to be his companions on the visitation of the diocese. The bishop now has the right to take any two priests he may choose, even those of the cathedral or collegiate chapter.

2) Canon 396 revoked the privilege of option in reference to the conferring of dignities in both cathedral and collegiate chapters, unless the option exists in virtue of agreements with the founder of the dignity or the canonry. By the option the senior canon could obtain the lowest dignity, and a lower dignitary could rise to a higher dignity.

3) Canon 403 revoked customs and privileges that permitted certain people to nominate and present candidates to canonries and benefices in cathedral and collegiate churches. The sole exception exists when the right of nomination or presentation for benefices or canonries in cathedral and collegiate churches is granted in the charter of the foundation of the benefice. With the exception of the dignities, the bishop has the right with the advice of the chapter to confer each and every benefice and canonry in cathedral and collegiate churches.

4) Canon 460 revoked any customs or privileges that permitted more than one pastor to have the actual care of souls in one and the same parish. This revocation did not affect the language parishes which were erected before the promulgation of the Code and sanctioned by the Holy See, as is evident from canon 216.

5) Canon 519 revoked all those privileges, once held by certain exempt religious organizations, by which their subjects could not validly confess to a priest not approved for the hearing of their confessions by the superior. It also revoked the privilege by which only a priest approved by the superior could absolve a religious from some sin or censure that was reserved in the religious order or congregation.

6) Canon 522 granted to a woman religious the permission to go, for her peace of conscience, to any confessor approved by the local ordinary for hearing the confessions of women generally in any church, public or semi-public oratory. This confession will be valid and licit, and any privilege which religious orders and congregations of women held to the contrary is revoked.

7) Canon 544, § 2, revoked the privilege of any religious order

or congregation by which the applicants were excused from the obligation of obtaining testimonial letters from the ordinary of their birthplace and also from all other ordinaries in whose dioceses they had stayed for more than one practically continuous year after the completion of their fourteenth year.

8) Canon 613 revoked all associated participation as a means of obtaining privileges. Those privileges which were obtained before the Code by such a means are retained.

9) Canon 654 revoked the privilege by which a male religious who had taken solemn or simple perpetual vows in an exempt clerical organization could be dismissed apart from the process of a canonical trial. Apostasy, running away with a woman, and marriage or an attempt to marry are the only exceptions to this revocation.

10) Canon 774 stated that every parish church shall have a baptismal font and that all contrary statutes, privileges and customs interfering with that right of parish churches are disapproved and recalled.

11) Canon 876, § 1, revoked those privileges which permitted priests, whether secular and religious, to hear the confessions of women religious and of novices without a special jurisdiction from the local ordinary.

12) Canon 964, n. 4, revoked the privilege granted by way of an indult to certain religious superiors by which these superiors could issue to the temporarily professed religious the needed dimissorial letters for the reception of major orders.

13) Canon 1157 revoked those privileges which permitted someone to consecrate or bless a place without the permission of the ordinary.

14) Canon 1267 stated that in religious houses and pious institutes the Blessed Sacrament can be kept in the church or the principal oratory only, and in the convents of nuns it cannot be kept inside the choir or enclosure, all privileges to the contrary being revoked in the same canon.

15) Canon 1356, § 1, abrogates any privilege or custom that exempted from the seminary tax or assessment any of the

personalities or entities mentioned in the same canon. Mention is there made of the *mensa episcopalis,* all benefices, all parishes and quasi-parishes, hospitals erected by ecclesiastical authority, sodalities canonically erected, church buildings that have their own revenue, and every religious house, unless the religious live solely on alms.

CHAPTER IV

Loss of Privileges by Renunciation

Canon 72. § 1. Privilegia cessant per renuntiationem a competente Superiore acceptam.

§ 2. Privilegio in sui tantum favorem constituto quaevis persona privata renuntiare potest.

§ 3. Concesso alicui communitati, dignitati locove renuntiare privatis personis non licet.

§ 4. Nec ipsi communitati seu coetui integrum est renuntiare privilegio sibi dato per modum legis, vel si renuntiatio cedat in Ecclesiae aliorumve praeiudicium.

§ 1. Privileges are terminated by renunciation after such renunciation has been accepted by the competent superior.

§ 2. Any private individual can renounce those privileges which have been conceded in his own personal favor.

§ 3. A privilege which has been granted to some community, dignity, or place, may not be renounced by a private individual.

§ 4. Even the community or body is not at liberty to renounce a privilege which was given in the form of a law, nor can it renounce a privilege if such renunciation would be prejudicial to the Church or to other persons.

Article 1. Renunciation of Privileges in General

Canon 72 treats of the loss of privileges by renunciation. In the first paragraph of canon 72 the general rule for the renunciation of privileges is given, and then there is added the *conditio sine qua non* that makes this renunciation valid: every renuncia-

[1] Translation for canon 72 is taken from Cicognani, p. 808.

tion must be accepted by the competent superior in order that this renunciation have its effect. The last three paragraphs of canon 72 describe the kinds of privileges that can be renounced, who can renounce these privileges, and under what conditions.

Renunciation of a privilege is the voluntary giving up of a right or power which a privilege conceded, or giving up the use and the power of using the things of which mention is made in a privilege.[2] It is an express renunciation if the renunciation is effected by means of words or signs which make known the will of the one wishing to renounce the privilege; it is a tacit renunciation if the owner of the privilege makes known his intention to renounce his privilege by means of his actions, such as, never using the privilege. Augustine, in commenting on canon 76 and quoting from Reiffenstuel, stated that when someone makes a tacit renunciation, it means that someone knowingly and willingly performs an act contrary to the privilege, either negatively, by not using the privilege when one could have used it, or positively, by doing the contrary of that to which the privilege entitled one.[3] By not using a privilege a person does not necessarily mean that he has renounced the privilege. Canon 69 in fact says that no one is obliged to make use of a privilege granted to him solely for his own benefit, unless an obligation to that effect should arise from some other source. Therefore the non-use of a privilege means nothing more than the mere renouncing of a person's use of a right or a privilege in a particular case, but not the renouncement of the right or privilege itself.

A privilege must enjoy some kind of permanence before it can be lost through renunciation. Therefore those privileges which permit successive application (*habent tractum successivum*), such as habitual faculties, can cease through renunciation. But those that have a momentary effect, and are given solely in the manner of a dispensation which takes away some bond or impediment, are improperly said to be renounced. Suarez taught that as soon as such a privilege has been granted it cannot be renounced, because what has been done cannot be undone, and what has been taken

---

[2] Suarez, *De Legibus*, lib. VIII, cap. 33, nn. 3-4,—*Opera Omnia*, VI, p. 375.
[3] Augustine, I, 168-169; Reiffenstuel, lib. V, tit. 3, n. 201.

away cannot return, at least not through the power of a private individual. Thus a privilege that takes away an irregularity cannot be renounced, because the person who received it cannot once again incur the very same irregularity from which he has been dispensed.[4]

ARTICLE 2. TYPES OF PRIVILEGES THAT CAN BE RENOUNCED

Paragraphs 2, 3, and 4 of canon 72 describe the types of privileges that can be renounced. The first type mentioned is the privilege that has been granted to a private person for his own personal favor, and paragraph 2 of canon 72 states that such a privilege can be renounced. It has been pointed out that no one is obliged to use a privilege that was granted solely for his own benefit.[5] It does not make any difference whether it is a personal, real, or mixed privilege; if there is no obligation arising from any other source, then the person can give up the use of the privilege temporarily according to canon 69, or even permanently by renouncing the privilege in accordance with canon 72. If a privilege has been given to a private person, but indirectly it is for the benefit of other persons, he would not be free to renounce it; for example, if a person has been given the privilege of the portable altar he would not be free to renounce the privilege, since it can be presumed that the grantor of the privilege intended that it be used for the benefit of other individuals besides the person who received the privilege.

Therefore personal privileges which have been conceded in one's own personal favor, as long as the obligation to use them or retain them does not arise from any other source, can be renounced. The Code cites in a footnote to canon 72 a decretal of Gregory IX in reference to the renunciation of personal privileges. Pope Gregory stated: "Any person can renounce that which is known to have been introduced for his advantage."[6]

---

[4] ". *quia non potest homo illam priorem irregularitatem in se iterum facere.*"—Suarez, *De Legibus,* lib. VIII, cap. 33, n. 1,—*Opera Omnia,* VI, p. 374.

[5] Can. 69.

[6] C. 23, X, *de regularibus et transeuntibus ad religionem,* III, 31.

However, it should be noted carefully that the legislation in paragraph 2 of canon 72 in no wise destroys the force of paragraph 1. So it seems that a grantee can continue to enjoy his personal privileges even after he has made the formal act of renunciation, but has not yet received notification that a competent superior has accepted the renunciation.[7]

If a group that forms a casual unit receives some privileges in a manner that is the same as if each person received the privileges personally, then each person would be free to renounce his privileges, unless they were granted for the benefit of others, as mentioned above. However, privileges granted to the persons cannot be renounced by one if the renunciation proved harmful to the other, or if one was granted his privilege dependently on the privilege of the other.[8]

Paragraph 3 of canon 72 rules that those privileges which have been granted to some community, dignity, or place, may not be renounced by a private individual. It is not stated that they cannot be renounced at all. It is stated that the private persons connected with the community, dignity, or place cannot validly or licitly renounce the privileges, since it is not within their power or right to do so. A privilege that has been granted to a community, dignity, or place concerns the public good, and only the whole community or moral body with the permission of their superior may renounce the privilege.[9]

Pope Innocent III severely rebuked the Archbishop of Pisa for permitting clerics to renounce their *privilegium fori* in civil causes and to select for themselves lay judges. The Pope said: "A public right is in no respect derogated by an agreement of private individuals. . . . It is clearly patent that not only unwilling but even willing parties cannot enter into an agreement to submit to civil courts, since this is not a personal privilege which can be renounced, but it is rather a privilege accorded publicly to the entire clerical state, which no private pact can derogate."[10]

---

[7] Cicognani, p. 810.

[8] Reiffenstuel, lib. V, tit. 33, n. 194.

[9] Schmalzgrueber, lib. V, tit. 33, n. 178.

[10] C. 12, X, *de foro competenti,* II, 2.

In another instance, also noted in a footnote to canon 72, Pope Innocent III condemned the practice of those clerics who, when guilty of injuring someone, then renounced their *privilegium canonis* in order to permit the injured party to mete out a physical punishment on the cleric. The Pope said: "Even though this is not a violent assault, yet it is injurious, since the canon was enacted not so much in favor of the individual cleric as in favor of the clerical state."[11]

Privileges which have been granted to a place or a locality and are enjoyed by all who live there or pass through the place cannot be renounced by anyone, since the right of renunciation is given to all those who may enjoy the privilege, and inasmuch as it would be impossible to get all these people together to renounce the privilege, it has the effect of no one being able to renounce it. But if a community has a privileged place within the limits of its territory, and this place was privileged for the benefit of the community, then the community has the right to renounce the privilege.[12]

If the privilege is enjoyed by the whole community, the renunciation would have to be put to some kind of a vote in which the whole community would in some way participate. This is usually done in a General Chapter, where certain members of the community attend the Chapter and vote by reason of their office, and the rest of the community is represented by delegates who are elected by all the members of the community. At the Chapter, unless the universal law or a particular statute explicitly prescribes a different course of action, that which has been voted for by the absolute majority of those who vote shall have force in law. If no absolute majority be obtained on the first ballot, a second is taken. If no absolute majority be obtained in the second, the relative majority decides in the third ballot. A privilege that belongs to a whole community would not be considered the vested right of each individual member, and therefore it would not be necessary that the renunciation of a privilege be approved by a unanimous vote. Canon 101, § 1, n. 2, states that matters which

---

[11] C. 36, X, *de sententia excommunicationis,* V, 39.

[12] Van Hove, *De Privilegiis,* p. 237.

concern all as individuals, must be approved by all. A vested right, such as the right of the individual voter to his vote, cannot be taken from someone except by a unanimous vote.

Privileges that have been attached to some dignity or office may not be renounced by the person enjoying the privileges, since the renunciation would be detrimental to the dignity or the office itself. Public interest demands that those privileges be preserved, so that a pact made by some private individuals will not abrogate a public right or law.[13]

If a privilege has been granted publicly to a community, dignity or place, it concerns the public good, and therefore can be renounced only by a public person who has the care of that community or moral body, or it can be renounced by the entire community or moral body with the consent of a superior who is competent to accept the renunciation. That permission is mentioned in paragraph 3 of canon 72. However, in paragraph 4 of the same canon a definite limitation is put upon this right of renunciation on the part of communities or moral bodies. Paragraph 4 states that even the community or moral body is not at liberty to renounce a privilege which was given in the form of a law, nor can it renounce a privilege if such a renunciation would be prejudicial to the Church or to other persons.[14]

In the first case a community or moral body cannot renounce a privilege which was given in the form of law that was properly promulgated and made binding on all for whom it was given, since the law depends solely on the will of the legislator. It is not postulated that such a law be accepted by the faithful, nor can it be renounced by them. Privileges that have been given in the form of a law are given *ad bonum commune,* and it is not permitted to private individuals nor to particular communities to renounce those privileges. Even if the privilege is enjoyed only by a particular group and not by all the faithful, it will not be permitted for an individual in that group to give up his privileges if these privileges have been received in the form of a law. The privileges that are called clerical privileges, such as the *privilegium*

[13] C. 12, X, *de foro competenti,* II, 2.

[14] Can. 72, § 4.

canonis, the *privilegium fori,* the *privilegium immunitatis,* and the *privilegium competentiae,* have been given in the form of a law, and therefore cannot be renounced even though they are enjoyed only by a particular group of the faithful.

An exception to the regulation of paragraph 4 of canon 72 may be found in canons 1451, § 1, and 1470, § 1, n. 1. Both of these canons deal with the right of patronage, which comprehends the sum total of the privileges which together with certain burdens are conceded by the Church to Catholic founders of a church, chapel, or benefice, or also to those who have acquired the right of patronage from the founders.[15]

These rights and privileges as well as the obligations were given in the form of law. Frequently the rights granted to founders were not used by them, or by their successors, to the best interests of the Church, and as a result the Code in canon 1450 abolished thenceforth the right of patronage, although it respected such a right whenever it had been acquired before the promulgation of the Code. Canon 1451, contrary to the legislation of canon 72, paragraph 4, encourages those who have the right of patronage to renounce the privileges attached to that right, and to accept in their place spiritual suffrages, even perpetual ones, for themselves, and the members of their family. Canon 1470 recounts the various ways in which the right of patronage is lost, and renunciation is the first way listed, even though the right of patronage was given in the form of law.

The privileges accorded in concordats will also be governed by the legislation of canon 72, paragraph 4, since the concordats and the privileges recorded in them are given in the form of law. Therefore it will be forbidden for those who are bound by the concordat to renounce the privileges granted through and recounted in the concordat. In practice, if the civil State wanted to give up or renounce a privilege contained in the concordat, it could make this known to the Holy See. The Holy See could make a tacit acceptance of the renunciation, and then by mutual consent the privilege would be considered abrogated.[16]

---

[15] Can. 1448.

[16] Van Hove, *De Privilegiis,* p. 239.

The second part of paragraph 4 of canon 72 states that a community or moral body cannot renounce a privilege if such a renunciation would be prejudicial to the Church or to other persons. Renunciation of a privilege would be considered prejudicial if it would cause either temporal or spiritual harm to the Church or to other persons. In this text the word 'Church' refers not only to the Church universal but also to a part of the Church, such as a diocese. And the words "other persons" are not qualified with any limiting clause, and therefore refer to all persons, physical or moral, public or private.

Reiffenstuel admitted that a community could renounce privileges when the whole community gave its consent. However, it was to be understood that this renunciation was in no way to be prejudicial to the Church, or to a third party, since no one was permitted to renounce the privileges of the Church. Generally, then, neither a community, nor a bishop, nor any moral person may renounce a privilege acquired in the form of law, if the use of it proves beneficial to the Church, or the renunciation proves harmful. If the privilege is not beneficial to the Church or to a third person, then the community or the moral person that has the privilege may renounce it.

No one can question the validity of a renunciation of a privilege when its continued use has become harmful to the Church.[17]

Ojetti (1862-1932), in commenting on the last paragraph of canon 72, holds that a privilege which is such that it cannot be renounced without prejudice to a third party evidently includes a right for that third party, and quite patently no one can renounce the right of a third party. Thus, for instance, a community which has obtained from the Holy See the privilege of exemption from the jurisdiction of the bishop cannot renounce this privilege, since that would injure the rights of the Holy See, to which the privilege of exemption directly subjects the community. Furthermore, it is to be stated as a general principle that no religious, not even the Superior General, can renounce privileges granted to his religious institute. Renunciation is a species of

---

[17] Reiffenstuel, lib. V, tit. 33, n. 201.

alienation, but even major superiors are simple administrators, and no administrators, even those who are constituted with full powers, have the power of alienation.[18]

---

[18] Ojetti, *Commentarium in Codicem Iuris Canonici* (4 vols., Romae: Apud Aedes Universitatis Gregorianae, 1927-1931), I, 303 (hereafter cited as Ojetti).

CHAPTER V

Loss of Privileges Through Intrinsic Reasons

The first two methods mentioned by which privileges are lost, namely by revocation and renunciation, are essentially dependent on a direct voluntary action on the part of the one who granted the privilege, of his superior, or of his successor, as in revocation, or on a direct voluntary action on the part of the one who is enjoying the privilege, as in renunciation. There are other methods by which privileges are lost. These are in a sense the indirect result of an action that entails the loss of a privilege. The following articles will treat of the loss of privileges resulting from causes intrinsic to the privileges in the order in which they are mentioned in the canons of the Code.

ARTICLE 1. LOSS OF PRIVILEGES THROUGH THE DEATH OF THE ONE WHO GRANTED THE PRIVILEGES

Canon 73. *Resoluto iure concedentis, privilegia non extinguuntur nisi data fuerint cum clausula; ad beneplacitum nostrum, vel alia aequipollenti.*

Privileges do not become extinct upon the grantor's loss of power unless they were granted with the clause: *ad beneplacitum nostrum,* or its equivalent.[1]

Canon 73 treats of the loss of privileges as resulting through the loss of authority on the part of the grantor. The canon first of all gives the general rule that privileges do not become extinct upon the grantor's loss of power. The privileges referred to in this canon include all the different types, such as favorable and unfavorable, generous and remunerative, and also onerous. And the ways by which the grantor may lose his authority will be different in so far as the offices which the grantors hold will be different. The loss of power by the pope could result only from his death or resigna-

[1] Translation of Canon 73 is taken from Cicognani, p. 813.

tion. The loss of power on the part of a bishop, of an abbot *nullius,* or also of a prelate *nullius,* could happen as a result of his death, resignation, transfer or removal. But no matter how their authority may have ceased, the privileges they granted in virtue of their office do not cease, since these privileges do not depend upon the power that granted them for their continued existence in the sense that their continued existence depends upon the continued support of the power that brought them into existence.

The usual exception, which arises when such a general rule applies, states that privileges will become extinct upon the grantor's loss of power if they were granted with the clause *ad beneplacitum nostrum* or its equivalent. This is entirely logical and consistent with the nature of privileges, since they are entirely dependent upon the will of the grantor as far as their being granted is concerned, and if the grantor places any limits or conditions on a privilege, then those conditions and limits must be observed, or the person will be working without the benefit of a privilege, for outside certain limits the grantor did not intend certain privileges to remain applicable. Equivalent clauses that indicate the loss of privileges upon the grantor's loss of power can be the following: *durante pontificatu meo, quamdiu mihi placuerit, donec voluero.* However such phrases as *ad beneplacitum Sedis, donec revocavero, ad beneplacitum Ordinarii pro tempore,* and similar ones will not mean that a privilege given with such an attached clause will cease at the loss of power of the grantor. In a footnote cited by canon 73 an example is taken from the old law to show the difference between such clauses as *ad beneplacitum nostrum* and *ad beneplacitum Sedis.* It reads thus: "If the Roman Pontiff grants you the favor of allowing you to retain during his pleasure (*ad suae voluntatis beneplacitum*) the benefices which you were holding at the time of your promotion, such favor by his death, which extinguishes entirely the *beneplacitum* of the pope, ceases by that very fact. But the contrary is true if the aforesaid favor is granted for the duration of the pleasure of the Apostolic See (*ad Apostolicae Sedis beneplacitum*). For in that case, inasmuch as the See itself does not die, the favor will continue permanently, unless it is revoked by the successor."[2]

[2] C. 5, *de rescriptis,* I, 3, in VI°

Reiffenstuel pointed out that, if a privilege is granted absolutely, without any conditions, it will not be lost through the death or deposition from office of the grantor. However, if the privilege or favor was granted with the clause *ad beneplacitum meum,* then at the grantor's death the privilege or favor would be lost, since his *beneplacitum* would cease with his death, as is quite evident. But if a privilege was granted with the clause *donec revocavero,* it will not cease at the death of the grantor, since the act of revocation is a distinct and positive action, and if the grantor did not revoke the privilege while he was living, it will remain after his death. Words such as *ad beneplacitum meum,* or *donec voluero,* indicate a perseverance of the will which is extinguished by death.[3]

Legislation similar to that which is found in canon 73 is enacted in canon 66, which treats of habitual faculties which are granted either permanently or for a definite period of time, or for a certain number of cases, and are considered privileges outside the law. It is stated that, unless they contain a direct statement to the contrary or were given to the bishop on account of personal qualifications, the habitual faculties granted by the Apostolic See to the ordinaries and to others mentioned in canon 198 do not lapse with the vacancy of the see on the part of the ordinary to whom them were given (even though he had begun to use the faculties), but they are transmitted to the succeeding ordinary.[4]

The fact that many privileges are obtained by means of a rescript makes it necessary to keep in mind also the rules governing the loss of rescripts whenever the loss of privileges is being considered.[5] Canon 61 has about the same legislation concerning the loss of rescripts as canon 73 has concerning the loss of privileges. It states that rescripts of the Holy See or of an ordinary are not rendered invalid by a vacancy of the Holy See or of a diocese, unless the clauses in the rescript indicate the contrary. The second exception in canon 61 decrees that a rescript will be rendered invalid if the rescript confers on some individual the power to grant a favor to particular persons mentioned in the document,

---

[3] Reiffenstuel, lib. V, tit. 33, nn. 169-170.

[4] Can. 66.

[5] Can. 62.

and the one who has such power under the rescript has not yet begun to use it when the see becomes vacant.

The exception concerns the power or the faculty conferred on some individual to grant a favor to particular persons mentioned in the document, and the power is still unused. The case concerns not a favor already granted (*gratia facta*) but one to be granted (*gratia facienda*) to the particular persons or designated petitioners mentioned expressly in the rescript.

Pope Boniface VIII in speaking of a habitual faculty, if it was to be regarded as a privilege superseding the law, spoke thus of its permanence: "Should power be granted as a favor to some one that, by virtue of Apostolic authority, he can appoint to a specified church some worthy persons, or that he can confer benefices whose conferring has legitimately devolved on the Apostolic See, even with the right from the same authority to restrain objectors by means of an ecclesiastical censure, this grant, which fittingly should be permanent, since it contains a special favor, does not expire with the death of its grantor even when the grant has not been implemented." The pope then furnished what now constitutes the basis for the second exception of canon 61. He stated: "Otherwise, if power is given to him for an appointment to be made in favor of some specified person, that power indeed does expire in every respect if the grantor dies when the grant has not yet been put to use."[6]

Ojetti did not feel that the privileges which are recounted in rescripts are restricted by the second exception mentioned in canon 61, which states that a favor or a privilege will be lost if it is a *gratia facienda* and the grantor dies or goes out of office when the grant is not yet put to use. Ojetti contended that the legislation contained in canon 73 permits all rescripts, whether of favor or of justice, of a favor already granted or yet to be granted, whether the grant has or has not been implemented, to remain applicable even after the loss of power of the grantor. The reason for this, so he taught, is that a favor once received is not lost by the death of the one who granted the privilege.[7]

---

[6] C. 36, *de praebendis et dignitatibus,* III, 4, in VI°.

[7] Ojetti, I, 304.

ARTICLE 2. LOSS OF PRIVILEGES THROUGH THE DEATH OF THE PERSONALLY PRIVILEGED PERSON

Canon 74. *Privilegium personale personam sequitur et cum ipsa extinguitur.*

A personal privilege follows the person and expires with that person.[8]

Canon 74 makes two statements concerning personal privileges. The first one is that a personal privilege follows the person. This means that if a person has received a personal privilege he may use the privilege anywhere in the world. Its use is not limited to a certain territory. It is usually the Holy See that gives such privileges, or someone delegated with this power. Any subordinate legislator could grant it only in those cases in which his jurisdiction in the matter, concerning which the privilege is given, is not limited to the territory that has been assigned to him. This is contraposed to a local privilege, which is always restricted to a certain territory. The second statement made in canon 74 is that a personal privilege is lost with the death of the one who enjoyed the personal privilege. It does not pass on to his successors if it was a personal privilege. Therefore in this it differs from the real privilege, which passes on to heirs and successors in the same matter.

The matter covered by canon 74 on personal privileges and that covered by canon 75 on real privileges is so closely connected that an explanation of the two types of privileges will be necessary in order to avoid confusion. Hostiensis in his *Summa Aurea* indicated a division of real and personal privileges that has been accepted by many commentators. He stated that a real privilege is a privilege given to some church, dignity, city, or to some place or to some persons in connection with a place (a shrine) or because of some object they have (a miraculous image). Such a privilege is perpetual; it adheres to the object or place and will not be lost unless the object or place is completely destroyed.

A privilege can be said to be singularly personal if it has been given to a particular person or to a group of persons who have

---

[8] Translation of can. 74 is taken from Cicognani, p. 814.

been named individually and expressly. Such a privilege could not be transferred to someone who succeeded them in an office, unless this was also expressed in the privilege, since the singularly personal privilege dies along with the privileged person.

Common personal privileges are those that are commonly granted to certain persons because of some particular reason or cause; they are not given to a particular individual person by name, but a person is granted the privilege directly by law or when certain circumstances or reasons demand that he be given the benefit of some privilege.

Hostiensis indicated two other classifications of privileges that could fall into the personal privilege category rather than the real privilege category. The first type is a privilege which as *singulariter et communiter corporale* belongs to some university, college or moral body in such a manner that all individuals who belong to the university, college or moral body may use the privilege. The last type is a privilege which *as communiter tantum corporale* belongs to a university and can be used only by those who act officially in behalf of the university.[9]

If privileges were to be put in a category in view simply of their ultimate destination, then all privileges would become personal privileges, since they are all ultimately given for some person's benefit. However, if they are judged by reason of the subject to whom a privilege is given (*subiectum cui*), a difference will arise which will divide privileges into personal and real privileges. By reason of this distinction a personal privilege is said to be that privilege which is conceded directly in favor of a person because of his own merit. A real privilege, on the other hand, is conferred directly and immediately on some thing such as a place, an office, an object and the like. The real privilege is entirely distinct from a physical person and will have only a mediate relationship by reason of some circumstance. This occurs if some person has in his possession a privileged object, or travels through some locality, or embraces some state, or exercises some office which has certain privileges attached to it. It can be said that in the first privilege —the personal privilege—the superior grants a favor directly to a

[9] Hostiensis, lib. V, tit. 33, n. 3.

subject; in a real privilege a favor is indeed granted, but only indirectly, that is, by means of another object.

In practice it will sometimes be difficult to tell whether or not some privilege is a personal privilege that has been granted in view of the person's merits, or whether it is a real privilege that has been granted to some person because of the office he holds, or in view of some object he possesses, or on some other title. Michiels says that four things must be examined if one is to determine whether a privilege is a personal privilege or a real privilege.

First the words of the privilege itself should be examined according as they are understood in the *stylus curiae* and according to the proper rules of interpretation. If the words have reference to an object or an office or a place without any mention of the person holding that office or object or place, then the conclusion can be drawn that it is a real privilege. For instance, if it is stated that the office of vicar general has immunity from the payment of the cathedraticum, then it is presumed that there is meant the office and not merely the person holding that office at present. If the words of the privilege are directed to an individual person and that person is pointed out by his individual qualities, then the privilege is without doubt a personal privilege. For example, the privilege states that Father Titus, born June 1, 1920, and now pastor of St. Mary's, Jersey City, has been granted the privilege of the portable altar.

Canon 66, § 2, in dealing with habitual faculties, which are considered privileges outside the law, states that unless they contain a direct statement to the contrary, or were given to the bishop on account of personal qualifications, the habitual faculties granted by the Apostolic See to the ordinaries mentioned in canon 198 do not lapse with the vacancy of the See on the part of the ordinary to whom they were given, but they are transmitted to the succeeding ordinary. Therefore with the exception of the cases in which the bishop received the faculties on account of personal qualifications, these faculties are considered real and not personal faculties, that is, they are attached to the office of the ordinary, and not to his person.

Not only the words of the privilege should be studied, but also the matter concerning which the privilege is given should be studied. For it may happen that a privilege will be given out as a real privilege, but inasmuch as it lacks perpetuity it will be considered a personal privilege. And in like manner, if a privilege is supposed to be a personal privilege and yet has the notion of perpetuity about it, then it will be considered a real privilege.

The intention of the grantor must also be considered, for if the reason for granting the privilege is principally the person himself or some quality about the person, then the privilege is considered a personal privilege. If the reason for granting the privilege is some dignity or thing or cause not necessarily connected with the person, then the privilege is considered a real privilege.

Finally, if there is still a doubt whether a privilege is a real privilege or a personal privilege, then the generally accepted rule for doubtful cases[10] must be applied: a favorable privilege will be considered a real privilege, since according to Rule 16 in the Rules of Law "it is fitting that a favor granted by the legislator should be permanent." This is also based on the general rule that real privileges are permanent and personal privileges are temporal. An unfavorable privilege on the other hand will be presumed to be a personal privilege, since an unfavorable privilege curtails the rights of a third party, and it is fitting that the curtailment be of a temporary rather than a permanent nature.[11]

Privileges that belong to moral persons seem to be the major exception to the general rules for discriminating between real and personal privileges. Personal privileges in general are considered as temporary in contrast to real privileges, which are considered as permanent. However a moral person is by its very nature perpetual, and yet enjoys personal privileges. If it is a collegiate moral person it will be made up of a college or group of natural physical persons. If it is a non-collegiate moral person it will consist, not of physical persons, but of property and resources which are separated from the ownership and control of other persons and

---

[10] Suarez, *De Legibus,* lib. VIII, cap. 3, nn. 17-19,—*Opera Omnia,* VI, p. 237; Reiffenstuel, lib. V, tit. 33, n. 16; Schmalzgrueber, lib. V, tit. 33, n. 37; Ojetti, I, 307.

[11] Michiels, II, 516-518.

dedicated to some religious or charitable purpose. In either case the moral person will be perpetual, so that the privileges attached to that person will likewise be permanent.

Canon 74 will find application as regards the privileges of such moral persons. The privileges of moral persons will follow them wherever they may go, and they will also be lost if the moral person ceases to exist. A moral person can become extinct when it is suppressed by legitimate authority or if it has not evinced any activity for a space of one hundred years. Thus, even though it is perpetual by nature, it will cease to exist and will lose all its privileges if it is suppressed. Likewise, if it has not evinced any activity for one hundred years, the moral person along with its privileges will expire. If at least one individual of a collegiate moral person remains, the rights and privileges of all the others devolve on such a survivor.[12]

Therefore, though canon 74 will directly and perfectly apply to privileges singularly granted to some physical person, nevertheless canon 74 will also apply to privileges granted to moral persons. Inasmuch as these privileges, although in themselves permanent, are possessed by physical persons who are members of the moral personality, these privileges will be lost through the death of these persons. Therefore the physical person will lose his privileges, so that they will not pass on to his heirs, but they will remain in the moral personality.

ARTICLE 3. LOSS OF PRIVILEGES THROUGH THE COMPLETE DESTRUCTION OF THE PRIVILEGED PLACE OR THING

Canon 75: *Privilegia realia cessant per absolutum rei vel loci interitum; privilegia vero localia, si locus intra quinquaginta annos restituatur, reviviscunt.*

Real privileges lapse with the complete destruction of the (privileged) thing or place; however, if the place is rebuilt within fifty years, the local privileges revive.[13]

Real privileges are understood to be those privileges whose

---

[12] Can. 102.

[13] Translation for canon 75 from Cicognani, p. 816.

immediate passive subject, in contradistinction to personal privileges, is not a physical person but rather a thing. Therefore as passive subjects of real privileges there will be included corporeal things, either movable, such as an altar, a rosary, a picture, or immovable, such as a church, a cemetery, a hospital, etc. Real privileges may also relate to incorporeal things, such as privileges that belong to an office, benefice, dignity, etc.

Local privileges are those real privileges whose immediate passive subject is a place or an immovable corporeal thing. It can consist of a certain determined territory such as a diocese, parish, or cemetery. It can also include buildings that are erected on a certain definite foundation, such as a church, a hospital, a religious house, a shrine, etc.

Canon 75 declares that real privileges are lost with the complete destruction of the thing or of the place that was privileged. Things and places are destroyed when they substantially cease to be what they were. The ways by which things cease to be are as diverse as are the natures of the things included in this category. Incorporeal things will cease to exist when something which forms an essential part of the thing will cease to exist or will be destroyed. For example, a benefice will cease to exist when all the goods that formed the benefice have been destroyed, or when the sacred office which formed part of the benefice has been suppressed by the competent ecclesiastical authority.

Corporeal things cease to be whenever their material form has been so changed that it no longer can serve its original purpose. For example, if the greater portion of the walls of a church has been destroyed, or if almost all the beads of a rosary have been broken, then the church or the rosary cannot serve its original purpose any longer.

Canon 924 refers to canon 75 in stating that the indulgences attached to a church do not cease if the church is entirely destroyed but is rebuilt within fifty years on the same or nearly the same spot and under the same title. The precise meaning of the words "*fere eodem loco*" was declared by the Holy See to be that the church is rebuilt on the same spot or at a short distance, for instance one hundred or one hundred fifty feet away; it does not mean that a church may be rebuilt simply in the same town or within the same parish limits without a forfeiture of the attached indulgences.[14]

Canon 924 also states that indulgences attached to prayer beads and other objects cease only when the beads or the objects are entirely destroyed or when they are sold. Therefore, if they are donated to somebody or used by somebody else besides their proper owner, they will not lose the indulgences. This is something new dating from the Code, since a Decree of Pope Alexander VII (1655-1667) of February 6, 1657, which had been renewed by each succeeding Supreme Pontiff at the beginning of his pontificate up to September 5, 1914, when for the last time it was renewed by Pope Benedict XV (1914-1922), declared that the Apostolic Indulgences were lost, if the religious articles were donated to others after having been used by the first owner. The Holy See was requested to declare whether the Code through canon 924 revoked those decrees, and the answer was that the contrary decrees were revoked and that the attached indulgences would be lost only through a total destruction of the indulgenced object or in consequence of its sale.[15]

A church does not lose its consecration or blessing unless it is totally destroyed, or unless the greater part of the walls collapses, or unless it has been reduced to profane (secular) uses by the authority of the local ordinary, as provided for in canon 1187.[16] Canon 1187 states that if a church is so dilapidated that it cannot possibly be used for divine worship and if all means for the repair of it are wanting, the ordinary may divert it to some decent use of a profane (secular) nature.

If the destruction of a place to which privileges were attached is effected in consequence of orders from a competent authority, then the privileges will not reassert themselves even when the place is rebuilt within fifty years. In a case like that the privileges along with the place would be destroyed, and not simply suspended in

---

[14] *Acta Sanctae Sedis* (41 vols., Romae, 1865-1908), XIX (1886), 93 (hereafter cited as *AAS*).

[15] S. Poenit., dubium, 18 febr. 1921—*AAS*, XIII (1921), 164.

[16] Can. 1170.

such a manner that they could later reassert themselves. However, if the destruction came by way of an accident, or through war, or in consequence of any other similar cause, then the local privileges will reassert themselves if the place is rebuilt within fifty years. If the privileges adhered to the very ground or pavement where this church or privileged building stood, then the privileges would not even be suspended until the place is rebuilt, but would continue to exist even after the church or the privileged place was destroyed.[17]

For the reassertion of local privileges it is sufficient that the restoration of the place be undertaken before the lapse of time, as it is stated in the Code, has occurred. It is not necessary that the erection of the church or the restoration of the place be finished before the duration of fifty years has elapsed. However, the restoration has to be substantially complete before the place will once again enjoy its previous privileges.[18]

ARTICLE 4. LOSS OF PRIVILEGES THROUGH A CHANGE OF CIRCUMSTANCES WHICH MAKES PRIVILEGES HARMFUL OR THEIR USE ILLICIT

Canon 77: *Cessat quoque privilegium, si temporis progressu rerum adiuncta sic, iudicio Superioris, immutentur ut noxium evaserit, aut eius usus illicitus fiat; item elapso tempore vel expleto numero casuum pro quibus privilegium fuit concessum, firmo praescripto can. 207, § 2.*

A privilege also ceases if in the course of time circumstances change in such a way that, in the judgment of the superior, it has proved harmful, or its use is illicit; if a privilege was granted for a definite period of time, or for a definite number of cases, it becomes extinct with the expiration of the period of time or the exhaustion of the number of cases, without prejudice, however, to canon 207, § 2.[19]

Privileges as well as laws in general affect future actions, so that it becomes readily possible for the circumstances which were

[17] Reiffenstuel, lib. V, tit. 33, n. 173.

[18] Michiels, II, 641.

[19] Translation of canon 77 is taken from Cicognani, 819.

closely connected with the granting of a privilege to undergo a considerable change in the course of time, and to a degree not anticipated by the one who granted the privilege. Therefore it is not surprising that through a change of circumstances and conditions the privilege which was useful and licit at the time it was granted can later become harmful and illicit. In fact, conditions and circumstances can change to such a degree that, if the grantor had been able to foresee this change, he would not have granted the privilege.

According to the earlier law, if a privilege proved harmful because of a change of circumstances, the privilege did not cease; it simply became revocable. An example of this is found in a written communication of Pope Alexander III (1159-1181) to the Abbot and monks of Dol, France, in which the pope revoked a privilege that had gradually become seriously harmful in its effects. The Abbot and the monks of Dol, France, had received the privilege of collecting tithes. They continued to use the privilege even after they had become enriched with possessions, and when the other monasteries which had to pay the tithes found compliance with the obligation to be harmful. The pope did not say that the privilege had ceased, but since it proved harmful he revoked it.[20]

The question that interested most of the later commentators was not whether a privilege that had become harmful could be revoked, but whether or not a privilege would cease if the final and principal cause of a privilege ceased. This cause was understood as the reason why the privilege was granted as well as the reason for its continued existence, and as the reason without which the superior would not have granted the privilege at all. Some of these commentators held the opinion to which the earlier decretalists had subscribed, that is, that the privilege did not cease even when the final cause of the privilege ceased, but that the revocation of such a privilege seemed fully called for.[21] Others felt that if the final cause of the privilege ceased, or if the privilege became harmful, then the privilege ceased automatically without the intervention of

---

[20] C. 9, X, *de decimis, primitiis et oblationibus,* III, 30.

[21] Hinschius, *Decretales Pseudo-Isidorianae et Capitula Angilramni* (Lipsiae, 1863), p. 817.

anyone.[22] The more common opinion, and the one held by most commentators up to the time of the Code, distinguished the cessation of the final cause into a negative and a contrary cessation. They said that a final cause ceased in a negative manner when the reason which prompted the grantor to grant the privilege had ceased, under circumstances namely when the continued use of the privilege was not harmful or unjust to anybody. In such a case they said that the privilege did not cease.[23]

If the final cause ceased in a contrary manner, it implied that because of a change of circumstances the privilege had become harmful and unjust. The commentators at this point subdistinguished. They said that the privileges which were given outside or beyond the law, and accordingly did not contravene the existing law, did not cease even if its final cause ceased in a contrary manner, since the beneficence of the grantor was a sufficient cause for keeping the privilege in existence.[24] Also those privileges which, though contrary to the law, were meant to be applicable simply for one action, or for one completed undertaking, did not cease, since their desired effect had already been obtained and in many instances could not be undone.[25] But those privileges which, when they contravened the law, had a recurrent or successive application did not continue to exist if the privilege had become illicit and unjust in its use through a contrary cessation of its final cause, since any privilege granted to do something illicit would be null.[26]

The present Code settled many of the controversies concerning this matter when it stated in canon 77 that a privilege ceases if in the course of time circumstances change in such a way that, in

---

[22] Suarez, *De Legibus,* lib. VIII, cap. 30, n. 8,—*Opera Omnia,* VI, p. 356.

[23] Reiffenstuel, lib. V, tat. 33, n. 187; *Schmalzgrueber,* lib. V, tit. 33, n. 166; Suarez, *De Legibus,* lib. VIII, cap. 30, n. 6 ff.,—*Opera Omnia,* VI, pp. 355-356.

[24] Reiffenstuel, lib. V, tit. 33, n. 185; Suarez, *De Legibus,* lib. VIII, cap. 30, n. 2,—*Opera Omnia,* VI, p. 354.

[25] Reiffenstuel, *ibid.,* n. 186; Suarez, *De Legibus,* lib. VIII, cap. 30, nn. 3-4,—*Opera Omnia,* VI, p. 354.

[26] Reiffenstuel, *loc. cit.;* Suarez, *De Legibus,* lib. VIII, cap. 30, n. 6,—*Opera Omnia,* VI, p. 355.

the judgment of the superior, it has proved harmful, or its use is illicit. This judgment of the superior will be similar to the judgment made concerning the morality or honorableness of human actions. The judgment of human actions is based not only on the object of the act, but also on circumstances that surround the act, and also on the intention of the agent. In like manner the morality and honorableness of a privilege depend not only on the object of the privilege intended by the grantor, but also on the circumstances that surround the privilege whenever it is used, and also on the circumstances that surround the privilege whenever it is used, and also on the object intended by the one using the privilege. Therefore, if there is a change in any of these circumstances, there may also be a change in the morality and the honorableness of the privilege. The judgment of the superior is to determine this.

A privilege becomes harmful if it causes harm to the public good, to the grantee, or to a third person, and also if the prejudice, for example, of an unfavorable privilege is so increased that it is not merely unproductive of good but really harmful to a third party. In other words, the circumstances surrounding the privilege have changed to such a degree that, if the circumstances which now surround and affect the privilege had been present at the start, the grantor never would have given the privilege. The Sacred Congregation of the Consistory, with the approval of Pope Benedict XV, on November 6, 1920, revoked a privilege that had been granted to some ecclesiastical colleges and seminaries of promoting their students to sacred orders without the dimissorial letters of their ordinaries. The Congregation said that the reasons for which the privileges had been granted had ceased, and therefore the privilege itself had duly to cease, so that the common law could be restored to a uniform operation.[27]

The use of a privilege will become illicit if in the course of time the use of a privilege would become an offense against the divine law either natural or positive. The grantor of privileges would not grant a privilege that will permit someone to do something that is illicit. Therefore, though it is fitting that a favor be per-

[27] *AAS,* XIII (1921), 259.

manent, and the Code itself states that a privilege is presumed to be permanent, it is also fitting that a privilege cease if the privilege has become unjust or illicit because of a change of circumstances.[28]

Canon 77 also states that the judgment of the superior is required for the cessation of a privilege that, because of a change of circumstances, has become harmful, or if its use has become illicit. There is question here whether the judgment of the superior is a condemnatory one, which would amount to a revocation of the privilege, or whether it is merely an authentic declaration, stating that the privilege has ceased because of a change of circumstances that made the privilege harmful and its use illicit. Most of the authors feel that it is a declaratory judgment.[29]

The competent superior who may pass such a declaratory judgment is that superior who has authority over the matter of the privilege, that is, the one who granted the privilege, his successor or his superior, or someone delegated by any one of these. If a subordinate presumed to make an authoritative judgment concerning the privilege, he would in a sense be making himself a judge of his superior. He is not therefore competent to declare that the privilege has ceased, since this judgment is reserved to the proper superior. However, even though he cannot pass judgment on a privilege, he may suspend the privilege of one of his subjects if that privilege has become harmful to others or its use is illicit, since it involves a violation of the law. In this instance he does not state that the privilege has ceased, but rather that the law must not be violated, and if the use of the privilege will be a violation of the law, then the use of the privilege will be prohibited.[30]

The judgment of the superior is not a revocation of a privilege, nor is it given in the manner of a judicial sentence. The question may arise whether or not a person may use the privilege in the internal forum before and until the declaratory statement of the superior has been made. Van Hove (1872-1947), quoting from

---

[28] Suarez, *De Legibus,* lib. VIII, c. 30, n. 17,—*Opera Omnia,* VI, p. 359.

[29] Van Hove, *De Privilegiis,* p. 279; Ojetti, I, 317.

[30] Van Hove, *De Privilegiis,* p. 279.

the first edition of Michiels' work, *Normae Generales,* stated that as long as the judgment of the superior has not been made, the grantee may, with a safe conscience, at least in the internal forum, use the privilege that has been granted to him.[31]

Michiels, in his second edition, rejects that opinion. He holds that the privilege cannot be used in either forum, whether the external forum or the internal forum.[32] He explains this by saying that the judgment of a superior is not a necessary condition for the cessation of a privilege, and his affirmation will not exclude the possibility of a previous cessation. Therefore, if a privilege has become totally and permanently harmful and its use is made totally and permanently illicit, there does not seem to be any doubt that the privilege has ceased by the principles of the natural law itself, which would not allow such a privilege to continue in existence. The very nature of law itself prohibits a superior from granting a law or a privilege which gives someone the right to harm others or to perform unlawful acts. It also prohibits a superior from sustaining a law or a privilege which, when given previously, was just and licit at the time, but later, through a change in circumstances, has become unjust and unlawful. Therefore if such conditions exist, it seems probable that the privilege will also be forbidden in the internal forum, even before the declaratory judgment of the superior has been made or received.

Canon 77 does not state explicitly that the cessation of the privileges which have become harmful or whose use has become illicit is perpetual or temporary. There seems to be the possibility that, if a change of circumstances which made a privilege unjust or its use illicit be only temporary, then the privilege itself will be only temporarily suspended and will remain inapplicable until, as was the case with local privileges, conditions have changed once again to such a degree that the privilege may reassert itself. The superior, who must pass judgment on the state of the privilege, may decide that for the present the use of the privilege is prohibited, since he may foresee that the cause of the cessation is only a temporary thing, and that therefore the cessation of the privilege must also be a temporary one.

---

[31] Van Hove, *De Privilegiis,* p. 280.

[32] Michiels, *Normae Generales,* II, 650.

ARTICLE 5. LOSS OF PRIVILEGES THROUGH A COMPLETE LAPSE OF THE TIME OR A FULL DEPLETION OF THE NUMBER OF CASES FOR WHICH THE PRIVILEGES WERE GRANTED

The second part of canon 77 states that if a privilege was granted for a definite period of time, or for a definite number of cases, it becomes extinct with the expiration of the period of time or the depletion of the number of cases, without prejudice, however, to canon 207, § 2. Thus the Code indicates two more ways in which privileges may be lost, namely, through the lapse of a predetermined time period and through a depletion of the number of the cases for which the privilege was granted.

A privilege granted for a definite period of time, if it is a temporary privilege, is not a privilege strictly so called, since a privilege in the strict sense is to be considered perpetual (canon 70). However, the superior at times does grant such a privilege.[33]

If the privilege was granted for a certain specified period, then at the end of that period the privilege automatically ceases without any further statement from the superior who granted the privilege. Its use beyond the duration of that period will be illicit and invalid, unless common error should intervene, or unless it concerns faculties that have been given for the internal forum, and these, through inadvertence, have been used beyond the determined time. The inadvertence is understood to be of someone who has received delegated faculties.[34]

Privileges granted in the form of rescripts will be governed by canon 38 in a determining of the time when the privilege will cease. According to canon 38, rescripts which grant a favor without requiring the ministry of an executor take effect from the moment at which the letters were issued; other rescripts take effect from the time of their execution. Therefore privileges in which a favor is granted absolutely and directly by the superior without the intervention of an executor and for a certain period of time take effect not only from the date of their granting, but from the very

---

[33] Cicognani, p. 820.

[34] Conte a Coronata, *Institutiones Iuris Canonici* (5 vols., Vol. I, II, 2. ed., 1939; Vol. III, 2. ed., 1941; Vol. IV, 2. ed., 1945; Vol. V, 2. ed., 1947, Taurini, Romae: Marietti), I, 116 (hereafter cited as Conte a Coronata).

moment at which they were issued, and will cease on the corresponding future day determined in the rescript.

Canon 34, § 3, n. 3, gives the rule for computing the time for factors that abide for several days, or weeks, or months, or years. The canon states that, if the starting point does not coincide with the beginning of the day, the first day is not to be counted and the time expires with the end of the last day of the same date.

There may arise some problem when two different rules are given for a determination of the time when a privilege will cease, but it does seem possible to reconcile canon 34, § 3, n. 3, with canon 38, so that a person may use the computation of time that is most convenient for him. If he actually does start using the privilege from the moment it was issued, then the remaining part of the first day must be counted, according to the regulations of canon 38, and therefore, on the final day for the use of the privilege, the privilege will cease at that moment of the day in which it was originally granted. However, if he does not use the privilege on that first day, and if the moment of its being issued does not coincide with the beginning of the day, then that first day is not to be counted, and the privilege will last to the end of the last day instead of to the corresponding moment when the privilege was originally granted.

A privilege which has been given for a definite number of cases will become extinct with the ultimate use that depletes the number of the cases. Its use after that will be illicit and invalid, unless common error intervenes, or unless the privilege was given for the internal forum and through inadvertence the priest has not noticed that the number of the cases has become depleted.[35]

The Church supplies jurisdiction both for the external and the internal forum in common error.[36]

Common error consists in the belief of all or nearly all the people of a place, parish, or community, that a man has jurisdiction when he actually does not. The fact that the person knows that he has no jurisdiction does not interfere with the validity of

[35] Can. 207, § 2.

[36] Can 209.

his acts if by common error he is believed to have jurisdiction.[37]

Therefore if a person has a temporary privilege with a delegated power of jurisdiction for the external forum connected with this privilege, the Church will supply jurisdiction when the privilege has ceased, if common error exists and if the person acts without properly delegated jurisdiction. In a case wherein the person does not know that a privilege has ceased, for the reason simply that the time period for which it was given has expired, or the number of the cases for which it was given is depleted, the Church will still act validly in the internal forum. Canon 77 refers in this matter to canon 207, § 2, which is concerned with delegated power that has been granted for the internal forum, and it states that any act performed through inadvertence after the lapse of the predetermined time period or the depletion of the specified number of the cases is valid.

There does not seem to be any restriction regarding the duration of the time in which canon 207, § 2, can be used with reference to faculties applicable for the internal forum. It seems that as long as there is inadvertence to the fact that the privilege has ceased, canon 207, § 2, will apply, and the Church will supply jurisdiction.

---

[37] Stanislaus Woywod, *A Practical Commentary on the Code of Canon Law,* revised by Callistus Smith (revised and enlarged edition, 2 vols., New York: Jos. F. Wagner, Inc., 1948), I, 94 (hereafter cited as Woywod).

CHAPTER VI

Loss of Privileges Through Their Non-Use or Contrary Use

Canon 76. *Per non usum vel per usum contrarium privilegia aliis haud onerosa non cessant; quae vero in aliorum gravamen cedunt, amittuntur, si accedat legitima praescriptio vel tacita renuntiatio.*

Privileges are not lost by non-use or by usage contrary to a privilege, if they are not burdensome to others; privileges which are a burden to others cease by non-use or contrary usage, if there is a legitimate prescription against them or if there is tacit renunciation of the same.[1]

Canon 76 lists two more ways in which privileges are lost, namely, through tacit renunciation and through legal prescription, and it also explains when and how a privilege is lost through non-use and through contrary usage. Legal prescription against privileges and tacit renunciation of privileges are altogether different ways in which privileges are lost, but both have this in common: they both have application in cases where there is a non-use of positive privileges and a contrary use in negative privileges.

The legislation of canon 76 is practically identical with what was taught by almost all the commentators in the period from the Council of Trent to the present Code, with a few exceptions as regards unfavorable privileges. The canonists of that period distinguished privileges into those that were not burdensome to others, or unfavorable privileges, and those that were burdensome to others and curtailed their rights, and commonly were known as unfavorable privileges. The privileges that were not burdensome to others never could be lost on account of their non-use or contrary use; nor could they be lost by way of legal prescription, since there was no one who was able to start prescription against them; nor could they be lost by way of tacit renunciation,

---

[1] Translation of canon 76 is taken from Cicognani, p. 818.

since in the faculties there was no mention of any obligation of using the privilege. As regards privileges that were burdensome to others, there was no agreement amongst the commentators. Some taught that the privileges that have successive application could be lost only by way of legal prescription, and not by way of tacit renunciation, since the non-use or contrary use of a privilege on the part of the privileged person did not necessarily mean that he had the intention of giving up the privilege completely, but it meant only that here and now in this particular case he did not wish to use his privilege.[2] Other commentators held the opinion that privileges which were burdensome to others could be lost not only by way of legal prescription but also by way of tacit renunciation.

Before commenting on the present legislation of the Code, one should further study the terms used in canon 76, in order to understand fully their meaning and their application. Tacit renunciation of a privilege may occur in two different ways, that is, through the non-use of a privilege or through the contrary use of a privilege. A privilege that is lost through its non-use must be an affirmative privilege which grants the execution of a certain action. This non-use of a privilege may also occur in two different ways. First of all it may occur when someone does not use his privilege, for the reason that there is not presented to him the opportunity for using his privilege. The non-use of a privilege in this case is of a mere negative kind. The same thing would be said of a person who did not perform a duty that obliges under precept, for example, attending Mass on Sunday, during that period of time in which the affirmative precept does not bind, for example, on ordinary ferial days as regards the obligation of attending Mass. It cannot be said that the person omitted to comply with the precept; rather, he simply did not perform an act or a duty which at certain times he is bound by precept to perform.

The mere negative non-use of a privilege does not destroy such a privilege. No matter how long the non-use continues, it will not

---

[2] Suarez, *De Legibus*, lib. VIII, cap. 34, nn. 3-6,—*Opera Omnia*, VI, pp. 382-383.

[3] Reiffenstuel, lib. V, tit. 33, nn. 180-230.

be sufficient to bring about the loss of the privilege, since it is not an indication of the person's will or intention to renounce the privilege. The non-use does not cause any harm to anyone, nor does it bring about a tacit renunciation, since the reason for not using the privilege arises from the fact there was no occasion for the use of the privilege. Therefore a person will continue to possess a privilege even though no occasion arises for using it.

The second type of the non-use of a privilege is of a more positive nature than the first. It consists in not using a privilege when the time or the occasion for which the privilege was given presents itself. Such a non-use could be the indication that a person wants to renounce his privilege. However, a certain condition must be present before the person can be considered to have renounced his privilege. The non-use of the privilege has to be voluntary, that is, the person has knowledge of the privilege and the occasion for using it along with the possibility of using the privilege, for if the non-use were not voluntary it could not be considered the will of the privileged person. Therefore if the person, when the opportunity offers itself, does not use his privilege because of sickness, absence, impossibility, or inasmuch as he was in some way impeded, then the privilege cannot be considered lost through that type of non-use.

However, according to the common opinion before the Code, there were two ways in which a privilege might be lost, and both were based on the fact that the privilege was not used by the privileged person. The first was by way of legal prescription, the other by way of tacit renunciation. In the first manner the privilege was lost without any action on the part of the privileged person, but rather as the effect of some law that set a time limit on the non-use of certain privileges, so that if the privilege was not used during that period of time when it was presumed that it could have been used, then it ceased automatically.

As regards the matter of prescription, two different types of privileges were pointed out. Certain ones concede something to the privileged person in respect to other persons, so that there results some kind of obligation or service on their part, such as the paying of tithes. Another type of privilege entitles the privileged person to do something which, considered as a privilege, does not involve any inconvenience or obligation on the part of anyone else.

Privileges of the first type, which redound to the prejudice of others, can be lost through legal prescription based on the fact that the privilege was not used by the grantee. Accordingly the ones who are prejudiced by the use of the privilege can invoke a legal prescription against the privilege. This can also be accomplished, as was mentioned above, when a law states that a person's non-use of such a privilege within a certain predetermined period of time will be considered as involving the loss of the privilege through non-use or by way of tacit renunciation.

Privileges of the second type, which benefit the grantee and do not cause any inconvenience to anyone, are not lost through non-use or through legal prescription. However, they can be lost by way of tacit renunciation, if such an interpretation according to law can be put on the non-use of the grantee. There is no possibility of the invoking of legal prescription on the part of anyone, since the privilege has no relation to anyone besides the grantee, and he could invoke legal prescription only to his own prejudice. Some specific law must decide whether or not the non-use amounts to a tacit renunciation, since the non-use is not a certain and infallible sign of such an intention on the part of the grantee. If the privilege was given under a certain condition and that condition has not been fulfilled, then that could be considered as a tacit renunciation. Likewise, if it has been given for a certain length of time and it has not been used, then it may be presumed that the privilege was tacitly renounced. In reference to the loss of a privilege through legal prescription it was necessary for the prescription to run for ten years if the one who possessed the privilege was present, or for twenty years if he was absent; for thirty years with reference to the privilege held by a monastery, and for forty years with reference to a privilege attaching to Church property.[4]

If legal prescription was not operative in a case, and if no predetermined period of time was set by law for the use of the priv-

---

[4] Suarez, *De Legibus,* lib. VIII, cap. 34, n. 19,—*Opera Omnia,* VI, p. 388.

ilege against possible forfeiture, then no lapse of time, whatever may have been its extent, sufficed to effect the forfeiture of the privilege which was left unused.[5]

The present Code takes this last principle and applies it to its legislation concerning the loss of privileges through their non-use or their contrary use. According to canon 76 the non-use of a privilege will not result in the loss of that privilege if there is no prescription or renunciation, since the lapse of time alone is not a factor in the Church for obtaining or losing privileges or rights.

Privileges which are not burdensome to others are, according to canon 76, not lost through their non-use nor through their contrary use. They are not lost through legal prescription, since the affirmative privileges do not impose a burden on anyone, and consequently there is no one who is to be freed from an obligation when no obligation exists; and the negative privileges do not offer anything to be gained by way of legal prescription, since they are not burdensome to others and therefore do not affect the rights of anyone. Through the non-use of a privilege or through its contrary use a privilege will not be lost, since the use of a privilege is not of obligation unless it is so stated in the privilege and unless there is a declaration that its non-use will result in the loss of the privilege.[6] Likewise, privileges which are not burdensome to others are not lost by way of tacit renunciation, for the intention of renouncing such a privilege is not presumed in view simply of its non-use or contrary use, and the renunciation would not be valid unless it was accepted by the competent superior.[7] In declaring that such privileges are not lost, canon 76 indicates that they are not deprived of their juridic force, since "what is granted by the ruler ought to be permanent." The grantee may have manifold motives for not using his privilege; and the non-use or the contrary use of a privilege may indeed argue its cessation, but it assuredly affords no proof thereof.[8]

The second part of canon 76 states that privileges which are

[5] Van Hove, *De Privilegiis*, p. 269.
[6] Can. 69.
[7] Can. 72.
[8] Cicognani, p. 818.

a burden to others cease by non-use or contrary use if there has arisen a legitimate prescription against them or if there is a tacit renunciation of the same. The non-use or contrary use does not of itself suffice for the loss of anyone's privilege, even if the privileges are burdensome to others. There must be operative a prescription which is legitimate and valid according to whatever is demanded by law, or a tacit renunciation on the part of the privileged person, before these privileges will be lost. A further study of legitimate prescription and tacit renunciation is in order, then, if one is duly to understand them as factors that bring about the loss of privileges.

ARTICLE 1. LOSS OF PRIVILEGES BY WAY OF LEGAL PRESCRIPTION

Prescription, as dealt with in Book III of the Code, Title XXVII, is a means either of acquiring goods and rights or of freeing oneself from obligations. The type of prescription that is found in the civil law of the individual countries is adopted by the Church as its own law in connection with ecclesiastical goods, due exceptions being made within the limitations indicated in canons 1509-1512.[9]

Prescription is a peculiar mode of acquiring rights or also the ownership of property through the possession of them for a period of time under certain predetermined conditions, or of freeing oneself from an obligation when a predetermined period of time has elapsed. The former is called acquisitive prescription; the latter, liberative or extinctive prescription.

It is considered by civil law as a mode of acquiring title to incorporeal hereditaments by immemorial or long continued enjoyment. Prescription is the term usually applied to incorporeal hereditaments, while adverse possession is applied to lands.[10]

Both the civil and the ecclesiastical law demand that certain conditions exist before a prescription may be considered legitimate. There are five conditions that are generally indispensable for the establishing of legal prescription: it must concern itself with some-

---

[9] Can. 1508.

[10] Henry C. Black, *Black's Law Dictionary* (St. Paul, Minn.: West Publishing Co., 1933), p. 1405.

thing that is prescriptible; actual possession must exist; some kind of title must be present; the prescription must run for the time predetermined in the law; and the element of good faith must never be missing.[11]

First of all the object or right must be prescriptible, that is, must lend itself to possible prescription. In general, most things whether corporeal or incorporeal, movable or immovable, public or private, are prescriptible, unless with reference to them prescription is prohibited by positive law. The Church lists in canon 1509 a number of things that are not subject to prescription. Therefore, even though the Church follows the civil law of a country on prescription, it must be remembered that the civil laws of each nation regarding prescription are canonized only insofar as they are not opposed to the provisions of canon law as enacted in the Code.

Canon 1509 lists eight different things that are exempt from legal prescription. Therefore, if a privilege is substantially made up of any of the things there enumerated, the privilege will not be lost through prescription, even though the privileged person does not use the privilege, or acts contrary to the privilege. The following are indicated in the Code as not being subject to prescription:

1. Whatever pertains to the divine law, whether natural or positive.
2. The things which can be obtained solely by way of Apostolic privilege. An example would be the privilege sometimes granted to priests to administer confirmation and minor orders.
3. Spiritual rights which lay persons are not capable of receiving, that is, when there is question of prescription in favor of lay persons. Therefore, a lay person could not by way of legal prescription gain a privilege that involved jurisdiction or a benefice in the Church.
4. The certified and incontestable boundaries of ecclesiastical provinces, dioceses, parishes, vicariates and prefectures apostolic, prelacies and abbacies *nullius*.

---

[11] Canons 1509, 1511, 1512.

5. Mass stipends and their obligations.
6. A benefice without a title, that is, without even a color of title to form a basis for the right to the benefice.
7. The right of visitation and of obedience, if the consequence would be that subjects cannot be visited by any prelate and are no longer subject to any prelate. The essential constitution of the Catholic Church declares that all members of the Church are subject to the Supreme Pontiff, the inhabitants of a diocese or the subjects of a religious organization owe obedience also to the head of the diocese or the religious organization. Canon law admits legal prescription in connection with the rights of subordinate authorities, but no prescription is or can be admitted in the Church by which one can free himself from the rights of every superior authority. The Church has admitted the exemption of certain religious organizations from the authority of the local ordinary by making them directly subject to the Holy See.
8. The cathedraticum, which is defined by the Code as a token or acknowledgment of the submission and obedience due to the bishop on the part of all legal ecclesiastical persons of the diocese. Legal prescription cannot operate to excuse one from the duty to pay the cathedraticum.

The second and third conditions that must be present in order to have legitimate prescription are possession and some kind of title. The Code does not give any legislation concerning these, so the legislation that is found in the civil law is to be followed.

The lapse of the predetermined period of time is the fourth condition that must be observed for legitimate prescription. Only a prescription of one hundred years' duration is valid in the case of immovable property, precious movable goods, and rights and personal and real claims on the part of the Holy See. Goods, property, and rights of any other legal ecclesiastical person can be acquired by way of prescription upon the lapse of a period of thirty years.[12]

The lapse of time alone will not prove sufficient for the loss of a privilege through non-use or contrary use. The prescription must run for the time set by law, and if the right or the privilege

[12] Can. 1511.

does not relate to the things mentioned in canon 1511, the civil law of the place must be observed. In many States in the United States the time of prescription for immovable objects was fixed by statutory regulation at twenty years, and for movable things at a considerably shorter term of years.

The fifth and final condition, and one of the most important, for legitimate prescription is that the prescription must be effected in good faith. Good faith is a judgment by which one prudently concludes that one justly possesses a thing as one's own without any violation of the rights of another.[13] The Code states in canon 1512 that no prescription is valid unless it is based upon good faith, not only at the beginning of the possession, but also throughout the entire period of time predetermined for the operation of prescription.

In the period before the Code there arose the question whether or not it was necessary or possible to have good faith in the effecting of prescription, especially when a person wished to free himself from an obligation. A distinction was made between two different types of obligations. The first type bound a person to do something or to refrain from doing something. The second type bound a person to suffer something, or to permit something which curtailed his rights, in consequence of some privilege held by a third party. In the obligation to do something or to omit something, good faith, as deriving through one's lack of knowledge of another person's right was not in question, for the obligations could be subject to legal prescription only through an omission of the act that the person was obliged to perform, or through the performance of an act that was forbidden. Thus in both cases the element of good faith was lacking.[14]

The statute of limitations as it existed in civil law was not admitted by many of the canonists before the Code. They felt that the mere inactivity of the creditor did not release the debtor from his debt, since he had no basis for making prescription operative in good faith. Either he had the intention of paying the

---

[13] Bouscaren-Ellis, *Canon Law, A Text and Commentary* (Milwaukee: Bruce Publishing Co., Reprint, 1949), p. 754.

[14] Reiffenstuel, lib. II, tit. 26, nn. 89-119.

debt, and that would have been contrary to the intention of freeing himself from the debt, or he had the intention of not paying the debt, and that would have deprived him of the good faith necessary for legal prescription. On the other hand, if the obligation consisted in suffering an infringement on his rights or in assuming some obligation when asked by someone else, then there was a possibility of starting prescription in cases of this type. The person was not obliged to act until asked to do so, and therefore as long as he was not asked he was not acting contrary to good faith. If the period of time ran its full course for prescription, he was indeed freed from all claims inherent in the right and privileges of the third party.

Other commentators felt that it was possible to have good faith in the operation of legal prescription against an obligation to do or to omit something, as long as no obligation of conscience was slighted.[15] The famous example was that of a person not paying tithes for a certain period. One person could have the privilege of collecting tithes, and another person, because of that privilege, would have the obligation of paying tithes. If the privileged person did not exercise his privilege, then the other party could invoke legal prescription and be freed from the obligation. Good faith could exist, since the legal prescription was based on the non-use of a privilege, and not on the refusal to pay a debt.

Good faith is required not only at the beginning of the term of prescription but during the entire time postulated for the prescription. However, if a person takes possession of a thing in good faith, but later begins to doubt whether the thing belongs to another, he can still remain in good faith even though the doubt persists, provided he has made diligent inquiry to resolve the doubt. The reason for this is that *"in dubio melior est conditio possidentis."* It follows that a person is not obliged, in view simply of an insoluble doubt which arises later on, to divest himself of a thing which he obtained in good faith.[16]

Good faith and all the other conditions mentioned are necessary

---

[15] F. Schmier, *Iurisprudentia Canonico-civilis* (2 vols., Venetiis, 1754), Vol. I, tract. 2, c. 5, sect. 3, § 3, n. 25.

[16] Van Hove, *De Privilegiis*, p. 99.

for the effective operation of legal prescription against an onerous privilege which the privileged person has not used, or when the privileged person has acted contrary to the privilege on occasions when he could have used the privilege. The good faith must continue throughout the whole period during which the legal prescription is operative.

No consent on the part of the legislator is required for prescription against privileges that are burdensome to others, since the right that comes from a negative privilege would cease through prescription in favor of the one who was prejudiced by the privilege. The right that comes from an affirmative privilege is extinguished by liberative prescription in favor of the person to whom the privilege was a burden.[17]

ARTICLE 2. LOSS OF PRIVILEGES BY WAY OF TACIT RENUNCIATION

In canon 72 the Code treats of the cessation of privileges by way of express renunciation. In that canon are indicated also most of the rules that govern renunciation. These rules will also govern the tacit renunciation mentioned in canon 76, when a privileged person loses a privilege which is onerous to others if he has not used it for a long time, or possibly even has acted contrary to it.

However, a problem immediately arises when the rules of express renunciaton are applied, since the first rule states that the renunciation must be accepted by a competent superior. The question is whether that permission or acceptance by the competent superior is also necessary for the tacit renunciation mentioned in canon 76. There is no uniformity among the present day commentators. Some say that the acceptance by the competent superior is necessary, while others say that the law itself furnishes a sufficient permission for a person tacitly to renounce, and indeed with full validity, an onerous privilege through the non-use or contrary use of the privilege.

Abbo-Hannan say that a tacit renunciation is presumed if the non-use of an affirmative onerous privilege continues for a notable period of time, e.g., ten years. Likewise a tacit renunciation is presumed if acts of use contrary to a negative onerous privilege

[17] Van Hove, *De Privilegiis*, p. 270.

are continuously performed over a long period of time. If all these conditions concur, then in virtue of the previous consent of the legislator, as given in canon 76, the renunciation is accepted by the competent superior as soon as one may presume that it was made.[18]

Vermeersch-Creusen say that a tacit renunciation is sufficient by itself, so that it does not need to be accepted by the competent superior. They point out that the general rule as given in canon 72, § 1, demands that a renunciation be accepted by a competent superior, but that in canon 76, where the renunciation of a privilege that is burdensome to others is in question, the law in anticipation of such a tacit renunciation accepts the renunciation beforehand.[19]

After it becomes quite evident from his actions that a person wants to renounce his privileges which are burdensome to others, the legislator acts in accordance with this presumed intention, according to Cicognani, and reduces the relation between the privileged person and the interested parties to the requirements of law.[20] This seems to indicate a very active intervention on the part of the competent superior in the acceptance of this tacit renunciation.

Conte a Coronata does not speak of the acceptance by the superior of the tacit renunciation of these onerous privileges. The renunciation is brought about after a period of non-use of the privilege, so that a renunciation is presumed. The non-use must be of a privative type, which means that the occasion, opportunity, and freedom to use the privilege were present, but the privileged person chose not to use them. Moreover, according to the same author, this non-use must extend over a period of about ten years' duration.[21]

Van Hove did not say whether or not the renunciation must be accepted by the competent superior, but he did say that the renunciation must be proved and not merely presumed, since a

---

[18] Abbo-Hannan, I, 107.

[19] Vermeersch-Creusen, *Epitome Iuris Canonici* (6. ed., 3 vols., Mechliniae: Dessain, 1937-1946), I, 162.

[20] Cicognani, p. 819.

[21] Conte a Coronata, I, 115.

person may choose not to use a privilege which he is not obliged to use and yet not have any intention of renouncing the privilege. Moreover, the renunciation must concern itself with privileges that can be renounced and with persons who are capable of making this renunciation. And since it is very difficult to decide in some cases whether or not there has been any renunciation, the privileged person will retain his privilege as long as there is any doubt.[22]

Canon 76 does not legislate how the tacit renunciation by the pivileged person is made known, but it is connected with the non-use or the contrary use of the privilege as stated in the canon. Michiels feels that there is a seeming inconsistency between canon 72, § 1, and canon 76, inasmuch as the legislator has stated in canon 72, § 1, that an express renunciation will not take effect until it has been accepted by the competent superior, while a tacit renunciation, which by its very nature is less certain than an express renunciation, will take effect even without being accepted by the competent superior.[23] However, he further states that the inconsistency is more apparent than real, since the legislator has decreed that the non-use and the contrary use mentioned in canon 76 are equivalent to the acceptance of the renunciation by the competent superior as mentioned in canon 72, § 1.[24]

This writer is of the opinion that the tacit renunciation must be accepted by a competent superior, or at least submitted to his judgment before it takes effect in such manner that the privilege can be considered lost. There are many reasons for this. First of all, unless there is some proof that a person has tacitly renounced his privilege he could always claim that he had no intention of giving up the privilege and that his choice not to use the privilege on some occasions was falsely judged as a renouncement on his part.

Secondly, a certain time element must be considered along with the tacit renunciation, since the tacit renunciation will be based on the non-use or contrary use of a privilege over a certain period of time. Roelker (1897-1957) was of the opinion that the same

[22] Van Hove, *De Privilegiis*, p. 271.

[23] Michiels, II, 629.

[24] Michiels, *loc. cit.*

time is required for liberation by tacit renunciation as is necessary for release by means of prescription.[25] But it seems the period of time does not need to be as long as that which is needed for prescription, since in this case the presumption is that the person is voluntarily renouncing his privilege in an indirect or tacit manner. Therefore the action lies on the side of the privileged person. It is not a case in which someone is trying to free himself from an onerous privilege. Accordingly it seems that a shorter period of time can prove sufficient. But how long must the period of non-use or contrary use of a privilege last before it may safely be presumed that the person has tacitly renounced his privilege? It will remain for the competent superior to pass judgment on the case and to decide, after having considered all the circumstances, whether or not there was a tacit renunciation.

Thirdly, there should be some kind of consent or permission for or acceptance of this tacit renunciation, since the renunciation has to do with onerous privileges which involve the rights of other persons. They have a right to know if and when they are released from the obligations and burdens they must put up with as a result of that person's privileges. If they know definitely when the privileges were renounced or when their tacit renouncement was accepted, then they will have some sort of protection from the demands of the person in the future, since without the intervention of the superior who could grant the privilege again a privilege cannot be revived if the renunciation has taken effect.

Acceptance of the renunciation, or the revocation of the privilege after a tacit renunciation has been made, is not the only condition that must be present for the validity of a renunciation. The renunciation must be based on a non-use or a contrary use that evinces the free and voluntary choice of the privileged person. In other words, it is necessary that the privileged person did not make use of his privilege when the occasion for using it was present, and that neither absence, nor infirmity, nor inculpable ignorance, nor any other reason prevented him from using it.

There should exist some external manifestation of the internal intention of renouncing a privilege. The mere presumption based

[25] Roelker, *Principles of Privilege* (Washington, D. C., 1926), p. 127.

on the person's non-use of his privilege would not be sufficient. Some special circumstances connected with the non-use or the contrary use that will signify the intention of the person must be present. For example, a person might have been given the privilege of receiving a certain tax. He has never collected the tax, and whenever the person who was obliged to pay the tax sent the money in, the privileged person always sent the money back. How many times must this happen before the privilege is lost? Some commentators felt that even one clear case of the contrary use of a privilege would be sufficient to prove that the person has renounced his privilege. This was held to be especially true where the people had taken an oath to observe the privilege.[26]

Finally, in order to have a valid tacit renunciation based on the non-use or contrary use of a privilege, the privilege must be among those which are subject to renunciation. According to canon 72, any private individual can renounce those privileges which have been conceded in his own personal favor. Therefore a private person may tacitly renounce those privileges which have been conceded for his own personal use, but which are a burden to others. Paragraph 3 of canon 73 states that a privilege which has been granted to some community, dignity, or place, may not be renounced by a private individual. Private persons connected with a community, dignity, or place, cannot licitly or validly renounce the privilege, since they have no right to do so. A publicly granted privilege, for instance in favor of some community, concerns the public good and can be renounced only by a public person who has the care of that community or moral body, or by the entire community or moral body itself. Therefore, no matter how many times or for how long a period of time private individuals in the community refuse to use a privilege or in reality act contrary to it, and even explain that their action is a tacit renunciation of that privilege, their action will have no effect on the privilege, and in fact they may continue to use the privilege themselves since their renunciation has had no effect.

In the final paragraph of canon 72 it is stated that even a community or a body is not at liberty to renounce a privilege which

[26] Reiffenstuel, lib. V, tit. 33, nn. 218-220.

was given in the form of a law, nor can it renounce a privilege if such a renunciation would be prejudicial to the Church or to other persons.[27] Therefore clerics would not be free to give up their clerical privileges, even though they might be a burden to others, since they have been given in the form of law to the clerical state. Likewise a community could not give up its privilege of exemption, even though it implies a curtailment of the bishop's normal rights, since it would injure the rights of the Holy See. This would be more detrimental to the Church than any curtailment of an ordinary's rights.

---

[27] Can. 72, § 4.

CHAPTER VII

Possible Loss of Privileges in Consequence of Their Abuse by the Grantee

Canon 78. *Qui abutitur potestate sibi ex privilegio permissa, privilegio ipso privari meretur; et Ordinarius Sanctam Sedem monere ne omittat, si quis privilegio ab eadem concesso graviter abutitur.*

A person abusing the power granted to him by a privilege deserves to be deprived of the privilege; and the Ordinary shall not fail to notify the Holy See of the grave abuse of a privilege which it has conceded.[1]

A privilege is abused when it is pressed into service beyond the limits for which it was granted. This is an abuse by excess. It is true that if a person is obliged to use a privilege and does not do so in so far as he can and ought, then it can be said that the privilege is abused through non-use or contrary use. But a real abuse consists in pushing the use of a privilege beyond its limits, for example, by using the privilege in a time, or in a place, or with some person or thing for which it was not granted. Comprised within the notion of its abuse is also any unjust or unreasonable extension of a privilege.

It certainly will be an abuse of a privilege if it is used as an occasion for sin, as when an exempt person through his privilege takes the freedom to sin or to do harm to another, not exactly under the pretext of using his privilege, but with a view to letting his privilege serve for the purpose of escaping punishment.

Someone also abuses a privilege when he acts contrary to the very ends of the privilege. Thus someone who has a benefice and has received permission to be absent from his benefice on account of studies is said to abuse his privilege when, in connection with a neglect of his studies, he occupies himself with fruitless occupations.[2]

[1] Translation of canon 78 is taken from Cicognani, p. 823.

[2] Suarez, *De Legibus,* lib. VIII, cap. 36, n. 4,—*Opera Omnia,* VI, p. 402.

During the middle ages almost all the commentators according to Reiffenstuel were in agreement that a privilege would not cease automatically on account of its abuse, unless the reason for the cessation came from another source, such as a law which stated that a certain privilege would cease as soon as it was abused. They also made the observation that an abuse was properly a defect committed in the very use of the privilege. Although a person could commit other crimes for which he became deprived of his privileges, that was not what was meant by the abuse of a privilege.[3]

Canon 78 of the Code states that a person deserves to be deprived of a privilege if he abuses the power granted to him through the privilege. The power here spoken of must be understood in its widest sense, so that it includes habitual faculties, indults, or rights acquired in virtue of the privilege itself. It is also quite clear from the words of the canon that a person does not automatically lose a privilege by the very fact that he has abused the power granted to him through the privilege, but rather he deserves to be deprived of the privilege, since he has used his privilege contrary to the intention of the grantor.

However the grant of the privilege may contain a warning against the abuse of the privilege in that it expressly states that the privilege will be lost if it is abused by the privileged person. The law itself has decreed in canon 2263 that an excommunicated person is forbidden to exercise the legally authorized ecclesiastical acts within the limits defined by law. He cannot be plaintiff in ecclesiastical trials, except in so far as canon 1654 permits it, and he is forbidden to discharge ecclesiastical offices and duties and to enjoy the privileges previously granted to him by the Church.[4]

If the use of a privilege is made to serve as an occasion for the committing of simony, the person renders himself liable to the deprivation, even perpetually, of his privilege. In a decree of the Sacred Congregation for the Propagation of the Faith concerning

---

[3] Reiffenstuel, lib. V, tit. 33, nn. 176-179.

[4] Can. 2263.

stipends for Masses to be celebrated on a privileged altar, this kind of abuse was condemned. The decree reads thus:

> Since in some missionary territories an abuse has crept in that priests to whom the Apostolic See has granted an indult of a personal privileged altar, or who celebrate Mass on an altar privileged in some other way, dare to demand from the faithful something in addition to the customary mass stipend, for the reason that masses celebrated on altars privileged in either way are more valuable for those to whom they are applied; the Cardinals decreed that the ordinaries or superiors of the above mentioned places are to be commanded to announce to the ecclesiastics, whether the regular or the secular clergy subject to them, that no one of them may receive by reason of this privilege, whether it be local or personal, a mass stipend in excess of that which the synodal tax or the custom of the place has established, otherwise he is bound to restitution; nay more, the privilege if personal is lost forever, and the missionary does not enjoy the local privilege when saying mass at a privileged altar, as was declared by the Sacred Congregation of Indulgences.[5]

When canon 78 treats of a person's abuse of the power granted to him through a privilege, it has reference to a serious and very grave misuse of a power or faculty granted through this privilege. If a person commits a minor transgression in this matter he would not deserve to be deprived of the privilege. The person, therefore, must knowingly abuse the power given to him through the privilege. Mere inadvertence would not merit for him a loss of his privilege. Even if he acted out of ignorance, it hardly seems possible that he should lose his privilege unless his ignorance was culpable and the privilege concerned a very serious matter.

The person will not automatically lose his privilege whenever he abuses the privilege, unless the law itself states that in certain matters there will be an automatic loss of the privilege, or if, by

---

[5] S. C. de Prop. Fide, decr. 13 aug. 1774—*Collectanea S. Congregationis de Propaganda Fide* (2 vols., Romae Typographia Polyglotta S. C. de Propaganda Fide, 1907), I, 507.

the very nature of the privilege, it will be lost when it has been abused. In the famous case of the clerics who had a privilege to absent themselves from their benefices for the purpose of studies, the studies then took the place of their services and they received their stipend in consideration of their studies. Therefore, if they did not devote their time to studies, it was an injustice for them to collect their stipend without any service. Suarez was of the opinion that in such a case there resulted automatically a deprivation of the privilege.[6]

Canon 78 does not specify the superior who is to deprive the person of his privileges if the latter abuses them, but it is reasonable to presume that only that person who granted the privilege, or his successor, or his superior, or his delegate, may revoke privileges in such a case.

In the second part of canon 78 the ordinaries are told to notify the Holy See of the grave abuse of a privilege which it has conceded. The ordinaries in this case are all the local ordinaries and their vicars as well as the major superiors of exempt religious communities. The term "Holy See" here means the Roman Pontiff or any of the Sacred Congregations or Roman Offices, according to the rule of canon 7. In order that there be no delay in the eradication of abuses in any serious matter, such as relative to the reservation of the Blessed Sacrament, the Congregation of the Sacraments in 1938 gave the power to residential bishops and local ordinaries to revoke the faculties granted to some church or private oratory of reserving the Blessed Sacrament there if there was any abuse of that privilege.[7]

---

[6] Suarez, *De Legibus,* lib. VIII, c. 36, n. 7,—*Opera Omnia,* VI, p. 404.

[7] S. C. de Sacramentis, instr., 26 maii, 1938, n. 10, d)—*AAS,* XXX (1938), 206.

CONCLUSIONS

1. In a case of doubt concerning the revocation of a privilege, a person may continue to use his privilege until the revocation is made certain (pp. 45-47).

2. Priests who were members of pious associations before April 1, 1933, did not lose their privileges and faculties as members through the revocation made by the Sacred Penitentiary on April 1, 1933 (pp. 52-55).

3. The majority vote of a community is sufficient for the renunciation of a privilege that belongs to the community. A unanimous vote is not necessary (pp. 65-66).

4. The superior who in view of some change of circumstances decides that a privilege has become harmful offers simply a declaratory statement that the privilege has been lost (pp. 84-88).

5. Good faith is necessary in the operation of legal prescription against an onerous privilege when the privileged person does not use it or when he acts contrary to it (pp. 97-100).

6. Privileges which are a burden to others cease by non-use or also by contrary use if a tacit renunciation is made of them by the privileged person, and if this renunciation is accepted by the competent superior (pp. 102-105).

BIBLIOGRAPHY

SOURCES

Acta Apostolicae Sedis, Commentarium Officiale, Romae, 1909-1929; Civitate Vaticana, 1929—

Acta Sanctae Sedis, 41 vols., Romae, 1865-1908.

Codex Iuris Canonici Pii X Pontificis Maximi iussu digestus, Benedicti Papae XV auctoritate promulgatus, Praefatione, Fontium Annotatione et Indice Analytico-Alphabetico, ab Emo Petro Card. Gasparri Auctus, Romae: Typis Polyglottis Vaticanis, 1917; reimpressio, 1934.

Collectanea S. Congregationis de Propaganda Fide, 2 vols., Romae: Typographia Polyglotta S. C. de Propaganda Fide, 1907.

Corpus Iuris Civilis, 3 vols., Berolini, 1928-1929. *Codex Iustinianus,* quem recognovit et retractavit P. Krueger, ed. stereotypa 10., 1929; *Novellae,* quas recognovit R. Schoell, et absolvit G. Kroll, ed. stereotypa 5., 1928.

Decretales D. Gregorii Papae IX, suae integritati una cum glossis restitutae, cum privilegio Gregorii XIII, Pont. Max. et Aliorum Principum, Romae, 1582.

Decretum Gratiani, emendatum et notationibus illustratum cum glossis, Gregorii XIII Pont. Max., iussu editum, 2 vols., Romae, 1582.

Hardouin, Jean, *Acta Conciliorum et Epistolae Decretales ac Constitutiones Summorum Pontificum,* 12 vols., Parisiis, 1714-1715.

Hinschius, Paulus, *Decretales Pseudo-Isidorianae et Capitula Angilramni,* Lipsiae, 1863.

Jaffé, Philippus, *Regesta Pontificum Romanorum ab condita Ecclesia ad annum post Christum natum MCXCVIII,* ed. 2, correctam et auctam auspiciis Gulielmi Wattenbach curaverunt S. Loewenfeld, F. Kaltenbrunner, P. Ewald, 2 vols., Lipsiae, 1885-1888.

Liber Sextus Decretalium D. Bonifacii Papae VIII, Clementis Papae V Constitutiones, Extravagantes tum viginti D. Joannes Papae XXII tum communes, cum suis glossis integritati suae restitutus, ed. Taurinensis, Romae, 1888.

Potthast, Augustus, *Regesta Pontificum Romanorum inde ab anno post Christum natum 1198 ad annum 1304,* 2 vols., Berolini, 1874-1875.

Schroeder, H. J., *Canons and Decrees of the Council of Trent,* St. Louis: B. Herder Book Co., 1941.

REFERENCE WORKS

Abbo, John-Hannan, Jerome, *The Sacred Canons, A Concise Presentation of the Current Disciplinary Norms of the Church,* 2 vols., St. Louis: B. Herder Book Co., 1952.

Augustine, Charles, *A Commentary on the New Code of Canon Law,* 8 vols., Vol. I, 4. ed., St. Louis: Herder, 1921.

Beste, Udalricus, O.S.B., *Introductio in Codicem,* 3. ed., Collegeville: St. John's Abbey Press, 1948.

Black, Henry C., *Black's Law Dictionary,* 3. ed., St. Paul, Minn.: West Publishing Co., 1933.

Bouscaren, T. Lincoln, S.J.-Ellis, Adam, S.J., *Canon Law, A Text and Commentary,* Milwaukee: The Bruce Publishing Company, Reprint, 1949.

Castropalao, Ferdinandus, *Opus Morale,* 2 vols., Lugduni, 1682.

Cicognani, Amleto G., *Canon Law,* 2. ed., Revised, Westminster, Maryland: The Newman Press, 1949.

Conte a Coronata, Matthaeus, *Institutiones Iuris Canonici,* 5 vols., Vols. I, II, 2. ed., 1939; Vol. III, 2. ed., 1941; Vol. IV, 2. ed., 1945; Vol. V, 2. ed., 1947, Taurini, Romae: Marietti.

Hostiensis, Cardinalis (Henricus de Segusio), *Summa Aurea,* Venetiis, 1570.

Michiels, Gommarus, *Normae Generales Iuris Canonici, Commentarius Libri I Codicis Iuris Canonici,* 2. ed., 2 vols., Tornaci: Desclée et Socii, 1949.

Ojetti, B., *Commentarium in Codicem Iuris Canonici,* 4 vols., Romae: Apud Aedes Universitatis Gregorianae, 1927-1931.

Reiffenstuel, A., *Ius Canonicum Universum,* 5 vols. in 6, Romae, 1831-1834.

Roelker, Edward, *Principles of Privilege,* Washington, D. C., 1926.

Schmalzgrueber, F., *Ius Ecclesiasticum Universum,* 5 vols. in 12, Romae, 1843-1845.

Schmier, S., *Iurisprudentia Canonico-civilis,* 2 vols., Venetiis, 1754.

Schroeder, H. J., *Disciplinary Decrees of the General Councils,* St. Louis: B. Herder Book Co., 1937.

Suarez, F., *Opera Omnia,* 28 vols., editio nova a Carolo Berton; Vols. V and VI, *De Legibus et Legislatore Deo,* Parisiis, 1856-1861.

Van Hove, A., *Commentarium Lovaniense in Codicem Iuris Canonici,* Vol. I, 5 Tomes, Mechliniae-Romae: H. Dessain, 1928-1939.

Vermeersch, A.-Creusen, J., *Epitome Iuris Canonici,* 3 vols., Mechliniae-Romae: H. Dessain, Vol. I, 7. ed., 1949; Vol. II, 6. ed., 1940; Vol. III, 6. ed., 1946.

Wernz, Franciscus X, *Ius Decretalium,* 6 vols., Vol. I, 2. ed., Romae, 1905.

Woywod, Stanislaus, *A Practical Commentary on the Code of Canon Law,* revised by Callistus Smith, revised and enlarged edition, 2 vols., New York: Jos. F. Wagner, Inc., 1948.

Periodicals

American Ecclesiastical Review, The, American Ecclesiastical Review, Vols. I-XXXII, Philadelphia, 1889-1905; *The Ecclesiastical Review,* Philadelphia, 1905-1943; from 1944, *The American Ecclesiastical Review,* Washington, D. C., Vol. CX, 1944—

Apollinaris, Romae, 1928—

ABBREVIATIONS

AAS—Acta Apostolicae Sedis
ASS—Acta Sanctae Sedis
C.—Causa
c.—caput
can.—canon
Cicognani—*Canon Law*
D.—*Digestum Iustinianum* or *Distinctio*
disp.—disputatio
Hostiensis—*Summa Aurea*
P. in Castropalao—punctum
p. in all others—page
Reiffenstuel—*Ius Canonicum Universum*
Schmalzgrueber—*Ius Ecclesiasticum Universum*
tit.—titulus
tr.—tractatus

BIOGRAPHICAL NOTE

Jeremiah F. Kelliher was born in Brooklyn, New York, April 7, 1926. He attended the local public schools in Kingston, New York, for his elementary and secondary education. In September, 1940, he entered St. John's Atonement Seminary at Graymoor, Garrison, New York. He entered the novitiate of the Society of the Atonement in July, 1944, at Saranac Lake, New York, and in July, 1945, made his first profession of vows. In September, 1945, he enrolled in the School of Philosophy at The Catholic University of America, and received his Bachelor of Arts degree in Philosophy in June, 1947. In the fall of 1947 he entered the School of Theology at the Angelicum University in Rome. He made his final profession of vows in Rome on July 14, 1948. On June 15, 1951, he received the degree of Licentiate of Sacred Theology from the Angelicum University. On June 17, 1951, he was ordained in Rome by His Excellency, Archbishop Venini, the secret almoner of His Holiness, Pope Pius XII. In the fall of 1951 he was assigned to the Faculty of the House of Theology of the Franciscan Friars of the Atonement in Washington, D. C. In October, 1952, he enrolled in the School of Canon Law at The Catholic University of America, and received the degree of Bachelor of Canon Law in June, 1953. In June, 1954, he received the degree of Licentiate of Canon Law.

ALPHABETICAL INDEX

CANON LAW STUDIES*

358. SESTO, REV. GENNARO J., S.D.B., A.B., S.T.L., J.C.L., Guardians of the mentally ill in ecclesiastical trials.
359. CARROLL, REV. JAMES J., A.B., J.C.L., The bishop's quinquennial report.
360. CURTIN, REV. WILLIAM THOMAS, A.B., J.C.L., The plaint of nullity against the sentence.
361. GANTER, REV. BERNARD J., J.C.L., Clerical attire.
362. GOERTZ, REV. VICTOR M., J.C.L., The judicial summons.
363. HEINTSCHEL, REV. DONALD E., A.B., J.C.L., The medieval concept of an ecclesiastical office.
364. KELLIHER, REV. JEREMIAH FRANCIS, S.A., S.T.L., J.C.L., Loss of privileges.
365. MOCK, REV. TIMOTHY, C.M.M., J.C.L., Disqualification of electors in ecclesiastical elections.
366. SMYER, REV. FRANCIS ANTHONY, A.B., J.C.L., Canonical regulations regarding exposition of the Blessed Sacrament according to canons 1274 and 1275.
367. WIGGINS, REV. URBAN C., A.B., J.C.L., Property laws of the State of Ohio affecting the Church.

*For a complete list of the available numbers of this series apply to the Catholic University of America Press, 620 Michigan Avenue, N.E., Washington (17), D. C., for a general catalogue.

www.ingramcontent.com/pod-product-compliance
Lightning Source LLC
LaVergne TN
LVHW050205080826
844660LV00012B/355

* 9 7 8 0 8 1 3 2 2 6 6 9 9 *